ORIGINAL
VW BEETLE

ORGINAL

VW BEETLE

LAURENCE MEREDITH

PHOTOGRAPHY BY PAUL DEBOIS
EDITED BY MARK HUGHES

FRONT COVER

A superbly original specimen. Nick
Carr-Forster's Beetle, almost
unblemished from new, was
manufactured in October 1956.

BACK COVER

The delights of fresh-air motoring.
Bob Wynn's Beetle cabriolet dates
from April 1964.

Published 1994 by Bay View Books Ltd
The Red House, 25-26 Bridgeland Street
Bideford, Devon EX39 2PZ

© Copyright Bay View Books Ltd 1994
Typesetting and layout by Chris Fayers

ISBN 1 870979 46 X
Printed in Hong Kong by
Paramount Printing Group

CONTENTS

BEETLE PAST & PRESENT

The Volkswagen Beetle is a true classic without peers. Many cars are certainly more powerful, more comfortable, more economical and better suited to modern driving conditions but, without exception, none holds the same fascination, has as much charismatic appeal, the same classless status or depth of character. The Beetle is unique. Few motoring folk have ever remained indifferent to the Beetle. Purely and simply, you either love it or hate it, but Beetles are best by far for the 21 million who to date have been persuaded to join the fold.

To the non-converted, all Beetles look alike irrespective of age, but there were in fact many thousands of modifications before German production ceased in 1978, due to the factory's policy of continuously refining the car and making real improvements where and when they were needed.

Until recently, only one item – the metal clamping strip that retains the bonnet and engine lid rubber seals – remained unchanged, but on the latest Mexican Beetles even this tenuous link with the past has gone, the seals now being attached to the bonnet and rear lid rather than the bodywork.

During the late 1940s, there was a concerted effort to make the Beetle more reliable. Improvements were made to the engine's cooling fins, thermostatically controlled flaps decreased the time it took for the engine to reach its optimum operating temperature, and cylinder life was extended by the addition of a higher phosphor content to the metal. Between 1945 and 1948, no changes were made to the bodywork, but by July 1949 there were visible alterations with the introduction of the Export or deluxe model. Gloss paint became available and the hub caps, bumpers, door handles and headlamp rims were chromium-plated.

Dawn of the Beetle's days as a big-seller. With the launch of the new Export model in 1949, Beetle sales escalated dramatically, climbing above 100,000 a year for the first time in 1952. This 1951 car, identified by the ventilation flaps fitted behind the front wings, illustrates how the Beetle's appearance in Export guise was enhanced by plentiful use of bright trim.

Into the twilight period. This gorgeous 1977 cabriolet with white vinyl trim and head restraints shows how plush the Beetle had become in its declining years. Although the 1303 model – with characteristic bulbous nose and MacPherson strut front suspension beneath – had ceased production in saloon form in 1975, it soldiered on as a cabriolet until 1980.

After 1950, so many changes were made that it is possible to identify Beetles year by year with a reasonable degree of accuracy, but problems frequently arise with 'rogue' cars that do not fit into an established category and whose specification, though genuine enough, appears to contradict official factory records. In such a case, it is not unreasonable to suppose that because of the mind-boggling scale of production at Wolfsburg, the occasional 'hybrid' would have found its way through the factory gates.

Problems over originality frequently occur where owners have, for whatever reason, carried out their own modifications. For example, after 1953, when a small oval rear window replaced the split type, some people decided to update their cars by removing the metal division in order to replace the two small windows with the larger oval, often in the interests of safety. For the same reason, older cars today can be

seen sporting more modern indicators because semaphores are not immediately visible in traffic, especially to younger drivers who were born long after these quaint items ceased to be commonplace.

It is far from rare to discover a 1950s bodyshell mounted on a much later chassis, but only the custodian of such a car is in a position to decide whether such a deviation from the original is sufficient to warrant major surgery. Other common problems of mixed identity involve cars that were destined for a particular country but found their way into a quite different one, cars that were launched in a new model year but fitted with the previous year's parts so that the factory could use up old stock, and cars that were converted to a previous year's specification by VW dealers whose more conservative customers would not accept new features as improvements.

So, if your 1966 1500 Beetle has 12-volt electrics

because the car was initially supplied to a doctor or a district nurse, or your 1968 1200 is fitted with sloping headlights, it may well be genuine and original despite the more generally accepted wisdom that labels your car as a wrong 'un.

Throughout its production life, the Beetle has been sold and driven in virtually every part of the planet including Antarctica and the world's remotest human habitation, Tristan da Cunha. Many export markets demanded a very different specification from that of the cars we are used to seeing in Europe and North America, body colour and seat cloth permutations alone running into many thousands. Back in 1985, the fact that there were 32,000 versions of Volkswagen's mid-range saloon, the Jetta, available world-wide serves to illustrate perfectly what we are up against in restoring a Beetle.

It is especially important for anyone who is restoring a Beetle to its original factory specification to establish the age of the car because Volkswagen's model year designation introduced for August 1955 continues to confuse even the most knowledgeable historians. Until that date, new model changes were usually announced at the beginning of January. Naturally, the Beetle was continuously refined and modified throughout the course of each year, but, by and large, the Volkswagen model year ran from January to December.

In 1955, the company established the August-to-August system of announcing new models to tie in with the factory's annual 'shut-down'. This is why, throughout this book, I have described the new model changes in the year in which they were announced. For example, the 1500 Beetle was launched in August 1966 and therefore appears under the heading '1966', but it was introduced for the 1967 model year and its specification was retained until August 1967, when a substantially modified and updated car superseded it. To put it another way, the 1967 6-volt 1500 was launched in August 1966 and the 1968 12-volt 1500 was originally announced in August 1967.

The system is easier to remember if you think of it in the same way that schools and universities organise their annual calendar. The new year starts after the long summer break, usually in September or October, and goes through to the following June or July. When ordering parts for your car, it will help enormously if you quote its chassis number and the month in which it was manufactured. Do not assume that because your car was manufactured, for example, in November 1972 that it is a '1972' car; it is actually a '1973' car because it was made in the 1973 model year.

Over the years, the Beetle has been singled out for customising more than any other make of car. There have been beach buggies, Bajas, 'rails' and many more, but by far the most successful and prolific fashion in recent times is the conversion of a standard Beetle into what is now universally known as the 'Cal-look' – the Californian look. Basically, it entails denuding the Beetle of its bright trim, painting the bodywork in a vivid colour, fitting alloy wheels, uprating engine power and lowering the suspension. Cal-lookers come equipped with non-standard seats, custom interior panels and a mega-watt stereo system, and in many instances the dashboard will have been transformed by skilful use of welding equipment and copious quantities of body filler in an attempt to create a 'smooth' appearance.

There is little doubt that several examples are masterpieces of modern automotive art, but a Cal-looker is not an ideal basis for a restoration project if you would prefer to own an original car. And a word of warning. The most popular method of lowering the front suspension is to cut the axle beam in two, fit an off-the-shelf device for adjusting the torsion bars, and weld the beam back together again. If the car you intend to buy has been treated to this particular 'tweak', the quality of the welding work should be inspected very carefully indeed. If it has not been done satisfactorily, you may not be able to drive your steed between the hedgerows for as long as you had originally planned.

It is also important to bear in mind that the Beetle was intended as an economical and inexpensive family car to be used for driving over many thousands of trouble-free miles. It was never intended as a precious museum piece and few have ever been treated as such. So, unless you are lucky enough to stumble across a one-owner car in immaculate condition, the slightly rusty hulk that pops and bangs every time you turn the ignition key is likely to be in need of a time-consuming restoration, or at least a little care and attention.

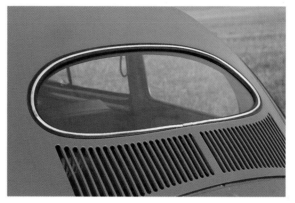

Together with its equivalent on the engine lid, the clamping strip retaining the rubber seal on top of the inner wings, seen on a 1947 car (above left), is the only part of the Beetle that remained unchanged throughout European production. Problems with originality frequently occur in the Beetle world. This is a genuine oval window from a 1953 car (below left), but some 1950s owners of earlier split-window cars updated them to look more modern.

BEETLES BUILT IN GERMANY	
Year	Quantity
1945	1,785
1946	10,020
1947	8,987
1948	19,244
1949	46,146
1950	81,979
1951	93,709
1952	114,348
1953	151,323
1954	202,174
1955	279,986
1956	333,190
1957	380,561
1958	451,526
1959	575,407
1960	725,927
1961	796,825
1962	819,326
1963	775,405
1964	867,328
1965	1,008,983
1966	988,533
1967	818,889
1968	1,055,529
1969	1,076,897
1970	1,014,819
1971	1,058,580
1972	914,030
1973	895,801
1974	451,800
1975	114,025
1976	87,463
1977	33,239
1978	790

With earlier Beetles, there are instances where enthusiasts have to ask themselves whether originality is more important than safety. Whereas the owner of this 1953 car (above right) has not altered the skywards-pointing brake lights, the owner of this 1957 model (below right) has chosen to add modern flashing indicators to supplement the normal semaphores.

Thanks to the huge classic car movement which has grown up over the past 20 years or so, restoring virtually any older car has never been easier. There are clubs, a wealth of specialist publications, companies involved in the manufacture of high-quality reproduction parts, and engineering firms well equipped to deal with all the problems you may encounter. And where spare parts are concerned, Beetle owners have a head start.

Because the car remains in production, the majority of bits and pieces you are likely to need, especially if you own a post-1967 12-volt car, are available from main dealers and independent specialists. The pre-1967 6-volt cars are a little trickier and even batteries are becoming difficult to obtain 'over the counter' these days, but even this situation need not deter a real enthusiast because, thankfully, there is a large army of VW nuts out there only too willing to

help you keep your car running in first-class order.

Beetle owners also have the added advantage that these cars are fairly simple in their construction. However, it is important not to under-estimate the high standards of build quality that went into making your car at the factory, so it naturally follows that restoring a car to such high standards will not be particularly cheap and certainly will not be achieved overnight. There are those who claim to have carried out a comprehensive restoration for just a few hundred pounds and I have listened with a great deal of scepticism to such drivel on several occasions. Indeed, I have seen their pitiful efforts all too often and have walked away with the inevitable conclusion that here is yet another Beetle tarted up with a glossy paint job to provide its owner with a fast buck. No restoration work is entirely useless though. Even the worst can serve as horrible examples.

Part of the purpose of this book is to serve as a guide for those wishing to restore a Beetle to its original factory condition. If Thomas Carlyle was right in saying 'The best effect of any book is that it excites the reader to self-activity', then this humble tome will have done its job.

Although the first production Beetle rolled off the Wolfsburg assembly lines on 15 August 1940 with the chassis number 1-000 001, our story begins in 1945 because until 1944, when American bombers had brought the factory to a virtual standstill, only 630 Beetles had been completed and they were used almost exclusively by senior Nazi officials, including Hermann Goering. Hitler also had a Beetle, but it is safe to assume that it did not get a great deal of use because he was unable to drive. Some examples of these early Beetles survive today, but naturally they are few and far between, and in most cases have already been restored by their enthusiastic owners. The chances of one being discovered in the proverbial barn covered in straw bales, unseen since 1942, are remote to say the least.

The cars that continue to be built in Mexico are similarly excluded on the grounds that they are probably too new to warrant restoration work. Mexican Beetle owners today, safe in the knowledge that the VW factory is working around the clock, can save themselves a great deal of work by purchasing a new one, provided, of course, they are prepared to join a six-month waiting list.

During the 35 years in which I have travelled in, driven, serviced, rebuilt, written about and generally 'mucked around' with Beetles, I have yet to come across two identical examples. All Beetles in my experience have individual characteristics that make each car special in some way. This is why the restoration and preservation of every remaining example is of paramount importance if, like me, you believe the memory and design legacy of the Beetle should live on in centuries to come.

Several of the highly-original Beetles featured in this book have had one fastidious owner from new. Vic Kaye still treasures the sales invoice of the 'World Champion' or 'Marathon' Beetle he bought new in May 1972.

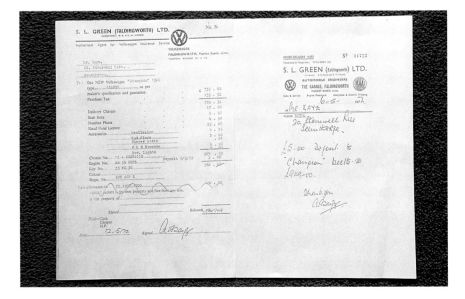

THE BEETLE IN 1945

I t is largely thanks to the British army that production of the Beetle resumed after World War II. With Germany divided into four occupation zones, the remains of the Volkswagen factory at Wolfsburg, under British control, had been hit hard by Allied bombing raids and lay in tatters. The workforce, which consisted mainly of German PoWs, worked long hours in conditions that today would be unthinkable, but there was little alternative because, although the factory lay in ruins, the machinery needed to produce cars remained intact.

An initial batch of 5000 cars was ordered for use by the army, which was by this time desperately short of motorised transport. Although the first 2500 Beetles were constructed by stretching the concept of improvisation to its limit, the future of the Wolfsburg Motor Works, as it was then known, looked promising. Production started by using whatever parts happened to be available and the cars that emerged before the end of 1945, fewer than 1800 of them, were necessarily crude. Production of the standard saloon (numbered the Type 11 by the British) began in August but just 58 units had been completed by the end of the year. There were, however, 703 'hybrid' cars built utilising saloon bodies mounted on *Kübelwagen* chassis (Type 51), which, having been originally destined for the German military effort, sat awkwardly high off the ground. Other cars produced during 1945 were either *Kübelwagens* or special-bodied cars ordered by the German post office.

Had the Beetle remained as it was initially, the car's

A beautifully restored 1943 Beetle (type number 82E) with a saloon body mounted on a Kübelwagen *chassis is typical of the wartime cars. Under the control of the British, the factory made a number of cars with the high chassis in 1945 and 1946 alongside the standard saloons simply to use up 'left-over' stocks. This Beetle, owned by Hermann Walter and painted army beige, is without hub caps but has the correct 'sickle' bumper overriders.*

future would have been by no means secure. The use of a fish-based glue in the interior trim, for example, gave rise to a horrible smell in the cabin, while the roof panels had to be welded together in two pieces and the oil coolers were prone to leaks. If the smell of fish did not grab you in the back of the throat, the acrid stench of oil burning on the crankcase and exhaust system certainly did. A steering box design fault also led to several serious accidents. But all these problems were quickly overcome and the long process of development began.

BODY

In addition to the inevitable beige and khaki used by the army, early Beetles were painted in matt black, matt blue for the RAF, matt grey for use by the American forces and maroon for a few (exactly how many is uncertain) ordered by the Russians. No cars were available to the public.

In keeping with Porsche's original design, the all-steel four-seater bodywork was bolted, as now, to the lightweight platform chassis with a central backbone for added strength and a rubber seal was seated between the two. The bodyshell is made from a number of individual panels welded together and comprises a roof, rear valance, rear luggage compartment, a rear crossmember which sits on and is bolted to the floorpan, two large side rear quarter panels which include the window 'cut-outs' and inner wings, and the sill panels that also conduct warm air from the exhaust heater boxes to the cabin through an outlet on both sides of the front footwells.

The front section of the bodyshell is made up of two sturdy inner wings that are joined in the middle by a valance, a luggage compartment floor, an apron that includes the rear and floor of the spare wheel well, a crossmember which, being similar to the one described above at the rear, also sits on and is bolted to the floorpan, and a large structure which comprises the dashboard, lower 'A' posts and the inner sections of the windscreen pillars.

From the rear, the early cars are distinguished by two small tear-shaped windows with a central vertical division, and below are 42 vertical air-intake louvres that allow the engine's fan to draw in cool air from outside.

The beautifully sculpted engine lid, hinged internally at the top, is pressed in the shape of a 'W' and includes an additional pressing for the registration plate, above which is the famous Pope's nose stop light. Below the registration plate is a simple handle for opening the engine lid and an aperture for the engine's starting handle, although the latter was rarely needed because an electric starter motor was fitted from the beginning.

The small tail lights, which glow with considerably less ferocity than a modern-day cigar lighter, were

Made in 'handed' pairs, the solenoid-operated semaphore indicators (left), typically dark orange in colour, are built into the B-posts. The classic W-shaped engine lid (below) and the 'Pope's nose' number plate light pod were to be modified several times, becoming less shapely over the years. The pressing for the registration plate itself disappeared in 1949. The bumper is rightly painted rather than chromed.

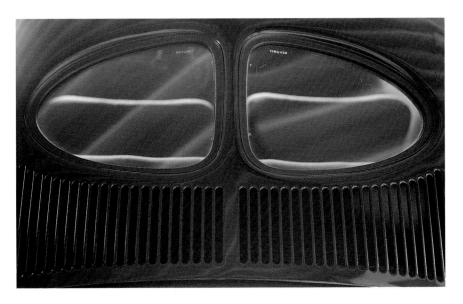

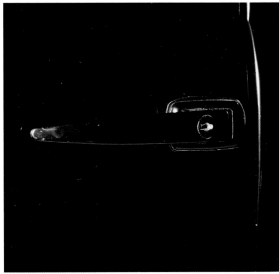

The 'split' rear window (above) was a prominent Beetle feature until March 1953, but the 42 air intake louvres were not changed in shape until the beginning of the 1958 model year. The door handles, like other items of external trim, were painted body colour (above right), and the one on the driver's side was lockable.

made in right- and left-hand pairs to take account of the curvature of the rear wings. At this stage, both the front and rear bumpers were painted in matt black or body colour, and were fitted with prominent sickle-shaped overriders. A single tailpipe sits below the right-hand half of the valance, but the exact position varies because these early cars were largely assembled by hand – some had a centrally-mounted tailpipe.

Up front, the bonnet, which had yet to receive a VW emblem or the Wolfsburg crest, is opened by a turning handle similar to the one used on the engine lid. Interestingly, the Beetle's bonnet is said by some to have been modelled on female genitalia, but my research reveals that this highly fanciful claim is not to be taken at all seriously. A large horn was mounted on the outside of the left front wing below the headlight, and the headlight rims, devoid of chrome at this stage, were usually painted in the same colour as the rest of the bodywork.

One particularly distinctive feature of early Beetles

is a small convex roof pressing, which was intended as a convenient base for mounting a radio aerial above the middle of the windscreen. It almost brings tears to the eyes, but someone recently told me of a man who, eager to achieve a perfect finish on the Beetle he was restoring, took a file to the roof pressing and flattened it out, thinking it was the result of accident damage – an almost irreparable piece of butchery which surely serves as a warning to us all against impatience.

The doors, which are front hinged, have pull-out handles externally, but at this stage only the left-hand door (the driver's side) is lockable from the outside with a key. Both the door windows are made in one piece without quarterlights and can be wound up and down with a conventional handle built into the interior door panel and situated directly in front of the door handle. Other external features include semaphore indicators situated in the 'B' posts and distinctive nipple-type hubcaps (painted rather than chromed) stamped with the VW emblem.

Not the result of a slip with a hammer (right), but a convex roof pressing intended as a base for a radio aerial. Due to shortage of materials, not all post-war cars had rubber coverings on the running boards (far right).

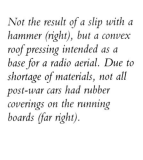

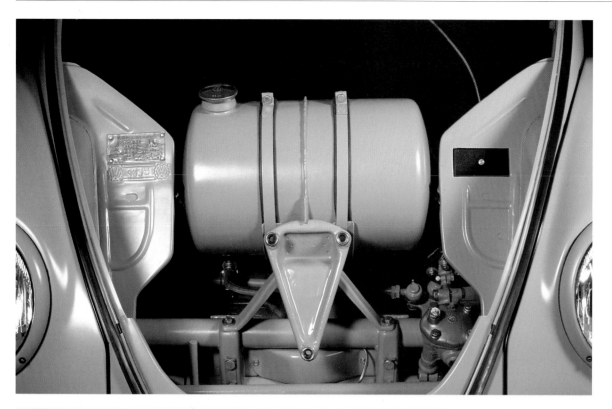

In 1945, the fuel tank became rectangular and acquired a much larger filler neck. The brass plate on the apron gives information about the car's weights and the body number – difficult to see on this black car – is stamped immediately below it.

The round jacking points fitted to early Beetles were found to be unsuitable as cars were prone to falling off their jacks when raised.

Under the bonnet, which is supported by a single sliding strut on the left-hand side, is a large rectangular 8.8-gallon fuel tank which, by 1945, had replaced the cylindrical type fitted to the wartime cars, and has a large filler neck on the right-hand side. In front of the tank, the spare wheel sits in its own well. Positioned on the body apron behind the wheel can be found a brass plate indicating the car's date of manufacture, its chassis number and the various weights, while the car's body number is stamped on the apron below this plate.

The four wings are simply bolted to the inner wings, a great advantage for the restorer who, it goes without saying, should never be tempted to save time in their removal by cutting the main bulk of the wings with a power chisel, merely to make it easier to loosen the retaining bolts – genuine early wings are now very rare. The steel running boards were usually covered in narrow-ribbed protective rubber.

INTERIOR

A model of post-war austerity, early Beetle interiors were not made with comfort in mind. The tubular frame seats were braced with lattice-work

The custodians of Beetles were lucky to get any kind of seat covering in 1945. In many cases, army personnel made do with a greatcoat stretched across the bare seat framework, but the more usual woolcloth is used here.

Some fore/aft adjustment of the seats is possible by unscrewing the wing nuts situated on top of the seat rails (below). The large, dome-shaped interior courtesy light (below right). Note that the headlining was confined to the roof panel on early cars, and did not extend to the metalwork around any of the windows.

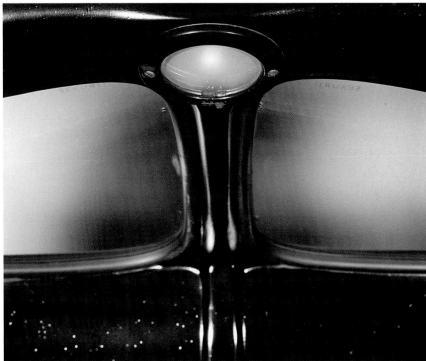

A headlining (right) was a luxury in 1945. Not all early Beetles had one because of a shortage of woolcloth in Germany. In the absence of a fuel gauge until 1961, there was a reserve petrol tank containing an extra gallon of fuel which the driver could call upon by kicking across the tap (far right) on the passenger's footplate above the backbone tunnel. Note the heater outlet on the sill.

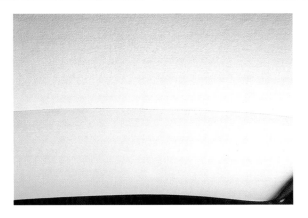

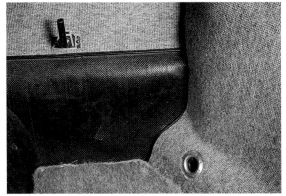

In typically Germanic fashion, the seats (above) are firmly sprung but give excellent support over long journeys. At first there was no heelboard beneath the seat. Interior door panels (above right) match the seat covers. The window winder is in front of the door handle.

An early speedometer is calibrated in kilometres per hour and the needle appears to run backwards. The steering wheel has thin, elegant spokes.

springing, padded with horsehair and covered in woolcloth, while the interior panels, including those fitted to the doors, were made of stiff cardboard and finished in woolcloth on leatherette.

Such was the desperate shortage of raw materials, however, that many cars – particularly those used by British army personnel – had no seat covers at all. Instead, soldiers were expected to use their coats to sit on. If you want to restore your Beetle to completely original condition, a couple of old greatcoats stretched across the front seats may well suffice but I wouldn't recommend such a rash course of action if you actually intend to use your car for the purpose for which it was intended.

Mounted on tubular steel frames, the front seats are secured in their guides by wing nuts, the loosening of which allows a certain amount of adjustment fore and aft. If he was lucky, the custodian of one of the first Beetles would have been treated to rubber mats in the front footwells and cord coverings over the inside of the front inner wings and front foot panel. The cloth headlining was fitted to the roof panel only, and did not extend at this stage to the 'B' or 'C' posts, or to the panel below the rear windows.

Most, but not all, early production Beetles had a cogwheel-VW emblem embossed on the black gear lever knob.

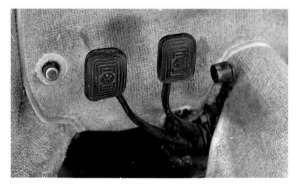

A small roller throttle pedal was fitted until October 1949, when, instead of changing to a conventional flat item, Volkswagen merely fitted a larger roller.

The austere dashboard (above) of the Beetles produced during the war changed little up until 1952. On post-war cars, an 'optional' radio would usually replace the embossed blanking plate to the right of the speedometer. Because this 1943 car is based on a Kübelwagen, it has a large, thick-spoked steering wheel, but, unlike the Kübel, it has a central horn button.

INSTRUMENTS & CONTROLS

The driver is confronted with an elegant three-spoked, thin-rimmed steering wheel with a centre push-button horn and the simplest of dashboards with minimal instrumentation. Naturally, all cars were left-hand drive and the steel dash, such as it is, consists of two stowage bins or gloveboxes made from steel (without lids) on the extreme left and right, a black-faced speedometer with white characters calibrated to 120kph to the left of centre, and a blanking plate embossed with the VW emblem to the right of centre.

A VW emblem also appears at the top of the speedometer. The ignition switch is located below the speedometer and the separate starter button is at the bottom of the dash. A black plastic knob at the top of the dash operates the indicators, while the light and wiper switches, also in black, are placed respectively to the right and left of the speedometer. A dome-shaped interior courtesy light is mounted at the top of the division between the rear windows.

Because a petrol gauge was not fitted, a reserve of

one gallon can be released by flicking a tap in the passenger footwell, a precarious activity for which a particularly adept right foot is required. So as not to upstage the left foot, the headlight dip switch was placed in the driver's footwell to the left of the clutch pedal, although quite why anyone would ever want to dip the feeble headlights of a 6-volt Beetle is open to speculation.

The handbrake lever is secured between lugs welded to the top of the chassis tunnel, and the straight gear lever immediately in front of the handbrake is topped with a black plastic knob which on some cars is embossed with the KdF cogwheel-VW emblem.

The brake, clutch and throttle pedal cluster consists of a base tube that also forms a mounting to the chassis. Cables for the clutch and accelerator are carried out of harm's way through the central backbone to the gearbox and carburettor. At this stage, a small roller ball suffices for the throttle pedal. Slightly forward of the gear lever on the right-hand side of the tunnel is the black choke button stamped with the letter 'L' for *Luftklapper* (air flapper valve); the choke cable also runs through the backbone.

WHEELS & TYRES

Between 1945 and 1952, all Beetles were fitted with 16in five-stud wheels made from pressed steel and initially painted with matt paint to match the body colour. Absurdly narrow 4.50-16 Continental crossply tyres were replaced by 5.00-16 boots in 1946, but these offered very little improvement in roadholding. After October 1952, more modern 15in wheels were fitted with 5.60-15 tyres.

Today, tyres are readily available for both wheel sizes. Whereas owners of pre-1952 cars are confined to using crossplies, post-1952 Beetles can be fitted with radials. Although radials would no doubt be frowned upon by out-and-out purists, they are generally cheaper and unequivocally a good deal safer.

ELECTRICS

Curiously, all Beetles up to 1967 had a 6-volt electrical system, the Bosch battery being housed under the rear seat on the right-hand side of the floorpan. Both the 1300 and 1500 models were equipped with 12-volt systems thereafter, but the 1200 model soldiered on with half a dozen volts even into the 1970s.

Due to a shortage of supplies, the first Beetles produced in 1945 were fitted with *Kübelwagen* headlights with vertical lenses placed awkwardly inside the wing pods. However, as things in Germany began to improve, the correct sloping headlights were supplied either by Hella or Bosch, and in most cases were stamped with a V-over-W emblem at the top or bottom of each lens.

At the rear, one bulb behind each of the two small red reflectors sufficed for the tail lights, while the single stop light was housed in the 'Pope's nose' number plate pod mounted on the engine lid.

Initially supplied by the German company SWF, the semaphore indicators were operated by a switch in the middle of the dashboard which activated a vertically-positioned solenoid in each of the 'B' posts. Made in left- and right-hand pairs, the semaphore arms were fitted with lenses which were a dark yellow-orange colour and usually 'ribbed'. Smooth lenses were employed from 1954.

The windscreen wipers are driven through a linkage by a small Bosch electric motor mounted in front of the dashboard under the scuttle. Several cars made throughout 1945, 1946 and 1947 were fitted with one wiper blade only – on the driver's side – because of supply shortages.

A Bosch electric starter motor with a solenoid was fitted from the beginning of production but a 'backup' facility was provided by a starting handle which, when threaded through an aperture in the rear valance, was placed directly onto the nut that also holds the crankshaft pulley in place.

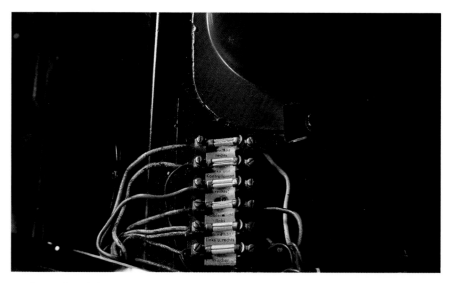

The coil and dynamo were also Bosch items. The dynamo, which sits on its own purpose-built alloy pedestal, is belt-driven from the pulley bolted to the crankshaft. A voltage regulator with an in-built cut-out sits directly on top of the dynamo.

Over the years, many Beetles have been converted from 6-volt to 12-volt systems, their owners weary of contending with the dreaded voltage drop. Six volts are fine if all are present and correct, but you have a problem on cold mornings when occasionally four decide to go AWOL. On the other hand, if you have a 12-volt system and four suddenly go missing, you still have eight, or two more than a six-volter on full song. I'm not suggesting for one moment that you upgrade your early Beetle merely so you can see when driving at night or get started on a winter morning. No, that would be far too easy. Six-volters are fun, so enjoy them for what they are.

Safety was not uppermost in Volkswagen minds when it was decided to mount the fusebox – containing six individually-labelled fuses – next to the fuel tank. Even the wiring on this car is original.

Well out of harm's way, the 6-volt Bosch battery sits beneath the rear seat on the right-hand side of the floorpan.

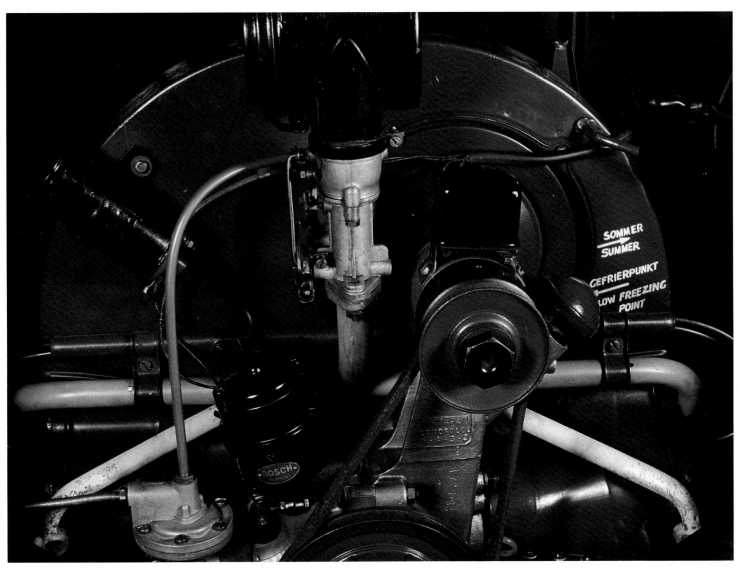

Largely hidden from view by the 'tinware', the 1131cc 25bhp air-cooled flat-four engine is a masterpiece of design, and its basic layout is still faithfully reproduced in Mexico today. Both the oil cooler and cooling fan are located in the sheet steel housing at the back of the engine, the fan being driven by the crankshaft pulley via the dynamo, which is positioned on top of the alloy pedestal cast into the crankcase.

ENGINE

The first production cars were fitted with the 1131cc engine originally destined for the wartime *Schwimmwagen* (amphibious car). This unit produced a maximum of 25bhp at 3300rpm from a 75mm bore and 64mm stroke, and a compression ratio of just 5.8:1. Due to a shortage of decent quality materials, these early power units were never particularly reliable and often required a complete overhaul within 30,000kms. In terms of design and layout, Mexican-built units remain unchanged to this day.

A neat and compact unit, the air-cooled, overhead valve, flat-four dispenses with a conventional sump, the normal function of which is catered for by a two-piece alloy crankcase split vertically on the centre line through the main bearings and simply bolted together. Long studs threaded into the two halves of the crankcase hold in place the finned cast-iron cylinder barrels and light alloy cylinder heads (mated to each other without gaskets) by passing directly

through them, the latter being secured on the outer ends of the studs by nuts. The combustion chambers are to a hemispherical design. Both the exhaust and inlet valves are 28.6mm diameter. The crankshaft runs in three main thin-wall bearings (steel-backed with copper-lead inserts) and one additional bearing that acts as a support for the auxiliary drives. The camshaft, mounted below the crankshaft and driven from it by single helical gears, operates the overhead valves via rocker arms and pushrods encased in cylindrical tubes, each cam operating two rods. At this stage the camshaft was mounted in the crankcase without bearings.

The flat-topped pistons are secured to the connecting rods with a floating gudgeon pin that is held in place by circlips. There are three rings on each piston, namely two compression rings and one oil control ring. Forged connecting rods are fitted with high tensile bolts screwed into the lower caps, while the thin-wall big end bearings are steel-backed copper-lead with white metal.

The wartime engines, although the same in principle, were intended for the Kübelwagen and differ from the post-1945 units in having a larger and lower air filter and a drilled crankshaft pulley wheel.

TECHNICAL OUTLINE

1131cc 25bhp
Cubic capacity
1131cc
Bore and stroke
75×64mm
Compression ratio
5.8:1
Carburettor Down-draught Solex 26 VFI or VFJ, HUF to March 1950, 26 VFIS to October 1952, followed by 28 PCI
Max power 25bhp at 3300rpm
Gear ratios (Standard)

1st	3.60:1
2nd	2.07:1
3rd	1.25:1
4th	0.80:1
Reverse	6.60:1

Final drive ratio
4.43:1
Gear Ratios (Export)

1st	3.60:1
2nd	1.88:1
3rd	1.22:1
4th	0.79:1
Reverse	4.63:1

Contained within the black-painted sheet steel fan housing is the oil cooler, which is bolted directly to the top of the left-hand crankcase. This simple but vital component contributed handsomely to early engine failures, many having been welded with inferior materials. To the right of the oil cooler is the cooling fan, which consists of a rotor mounted on one end of the dynamo armature shaft and driven by the fan belt at the other end.

The fan, which revolves at twice the speed of the engine, draws in air through the louvres in the bodywork above the engine lid and forces it over the oil cooler, cylinder barrels and heads. Critical to the cooling process, there are steel ducting trays (commonly referred to as 'the tinware') placed over the cylinder barrels and heads to prevent hot air from the engine finding its way into the engine compartment and causing overheating. Hot air from the engine is

Has there ever been a simpler carburettor? At first, Volkswagen made its own aluminium alloy carburettor for the Beetle, but Solex-made substitutes soon arrived and continued until the end of production.

expelled at the rear of the car below the valance but is also used for heating the cabin.

The distributor, driven by spiral gears from the crankshaft, is also located on top of the left-hand half of the crankcase. The diaphragm petrol pump, mounted to the left of the distributor, houses an operating rod driven by a cam on the distributor driveshaft which, in turn, is driven by the crankshaft.

Because the carburettor manufacturer, Solex, had its factory in Berlin which fell under the control of the Russians after the war, Volkswagen made its own carburettors initially. The small downdraught unit die-cast in aluminium alloy (Type 26 VFI or VFJ) is as rudimentary as any carburettor in the history of the motor car, consisting of a body and float chamber topped with a pancake air filter. The smaller components such as the jets were made by Voigtländer, better known as manufacturers of camera equipment. Petrol is dispensed to the cylinder heads through the extraordinarily long, small-bore inlet manifold so beloved of Beetle folk on cold mornings, when the engine refuses to run properly, due to the perennial problem of icing, until it reaches its optimum operating temperature. Made of steel and painted in grey or black, the manifold branches from a single pipe into two just below the carburettor. Each pipe is bolted to the top surface of the cylinder heads and feeds the petrol/air mixture into a single port in each head.

Engine oil is drawn from the bottom of the crankcase, which also houses a removable gauze filter, through to a gear-type oil pump situated in the rear of the crankcase and driven by the camshaft. Oil is pushed through holes in the case to the crankshaft, camshaft and pushrods, the latter also carrying lubricant to the rocker arms. The pushrods are protected by tubes that also act as conduits for lubricating oil. Oilways are also drilled into the crankshaft to connect the main journals with the big-end bearings.

Naturally, an air-cooled engine relies just as much on oil to keep it operating at the correct temperature, and conventional wisdom dictates that a monograde is preferable to a modern multigrade oil. Whichever you choose, all 4½ pints of it should be changed religiously at 3000-mile intervals.

From the outset, the Beetle was fitted with a heater. Heater boxes integrated into the exhaust system utilise warm air passed over the cylinder barrels and feed it into the cabin under the rear seats via pipes which divert air through the sills and into the front footwells. The earliest cars have the disadvantage that the heater control switch is located in the engine compartment next to the oil dipstick, rather than on the transmission tunnel as was the case with the later cars.

One of the endearing features of all Beetles up to the introduction of the 1500 model is the remarkable amount of space in the engine compartment, allowing easy servicing and maintenance. Everything, including the plugs, is within easy reach, making the Beetle a joy for the DIY mechanic.

TRANSMISSION

The gearbox is bolted to the rear of the chassis pan and to the engine, and is protected by rubber mountings against vibrations produced by engine torque. It also carries the starter motor on the top right-hand side. Split vertically and longitudinally, the ribbed, alloy-cased gearbox and final drive assembly are integrated into one compact and rigid unit. The gearbox, which is without synchromesh at this stage, is driven from the engine by an input shaft, and a Fichtel & Sachs 180mm single-plate dry clutch is splined to the input shaft.

The two friction surfaces are applied to the flywheel (which is bolted to what Volkswagen owners usually refer to as the front of the engine) and to the pressure plate which is fitted to the clutch cover. Positioned behind the centre line of the rear axles, the clutch is operated by an adjustable cable and contained within the bellhousing of the gearbox. When the clutch pedal is operated, a thrust ring makes contact with the clutch release plate which, in turn, disengages the clutch plate from the flywheel.

An integral part of the gearbox, the differential assembly consists of a differential housing with housing covers, side gears, pinions with pinion shafts, and solid axle shafts which are articulated with universal joints and contained within axle tubes. Both rear axle shafts are flattened on their inner ends and are fitted between fulcrum plates in the side gears.

The sliding nature of the axles in between the fulcrum plates in conjunction with the rocking of the fulcrum plates in the side gears allows the universal joints to work: a simple but exceptionally strong design which is almost, but not quite, unbreakable.

CHASSIS

A Beetle's rolling chassis (except for the later MacPherson strut cars) can be driven without the body *in situ,* for it is an immensely strong self-contained unit rather like a kart. Two floorpans, ribbed for additional strength, are welded to a central backbone or tunnel which also acts as a conduit for the fuel line, gearchange rod, throttle, clutch and choke cables. At the rear, there is a sturdy fork to which the gearbox is bolted.

All four wheels are independently sprung by transversely mounted torsion bars which, over the years, were 'softened up' considerably in the interest of ride comfort. At the front, the torsion bars are contained within two cylindrical tubes with five leaves in the top one and four in the lower one and are joined together in the middle by a pinchbolt.

Several torsion leaves were employed in two tubes rather than one torsion bar in each tube for many reasons. Firstly, leaves are cheaper to make, which was an important consideration in the 1930s when Dr Porsche was commissioned to design the Volkswagen, and secondly, they are very much heavier, a factor which partially contributed to balancing the rear weight bias of the car. Fitting two torsion tubes to the front axle assembly also offered a convenient anchorage point for the upper and lower parallel trailing arms, which are secured to the square ends of the torsion leaves with screws and nuts. The trailing arms on early cars were welded in a solid block to the outer ends of the tubes.

Cornering forces imposed on the trailing arms are taken up by the torsion leaves, while the vertically-mounted shock absorbers are bolted at the top of the steel uprights welded to the beam, and bolted at the bottom to a mounting stud on the lower trailing arms that points inwards to the car. The trailing arms are connected to the hub and spindle assemblies via a king pin and two link pins each side, and are held in place by bolts. The front suspension assembly is bolted directly, with four bolts, to the head of the chassis frame.

The two rear torsion bars are also contained in cylindrical tubes welded to and transversely mounted across the chassis in front of the gearbox. Being some distance away from the hub assembly and axle tubes, the torsion bar tubes are linked to the axle tubes by a single steel blade or radius arm each side. The torsion bars themselves, solid pieces of exceptionally strong but light cylindrical metal, are splined on their outer ends to allow for the fitment of the steel radius arms. Damping is taken care of by Hemscheidt lever-type single acting shock absorbers, but more modern telescopic units were employed after April 1951.

Drive from the gearbox to the rear wheels is taken up through swinging half axles which also run in

cylindrical tubes, an ingenious system eventually employed on such exotica as the Mercedes-Benz 300SL 'Gullwing' but one which quickly gained a reputation for creating unpredictable changes in rear wheel camber during hard cornering. Under extreme circumstances, the inherent tendency of the Beetle to oversteer could become almost uncontrollable, especially if one wheel adopted the dreaded 'tuck-in' position. The inclination of these early cars to invert themselves, however, has as much to do with the absurdly narrow 49in rear track and 4.50-16 cross-ply tyres as the general geometrical layout of the rear suspension.

Treated with a degree of respect for their limitations, the 1940s Beetles can be enjoyed at reasonably high speeds, even though their cable-operated brakes might give you food for thought in modern driving

Classic Porsche-designed front suspension (top) is by transverse torsion bars and parallel trailing arms. The conventional drum brakes are cable-operated and have a five-bolt wheel fixing. Rear suspension (above) is also by transverse torsion bars and trailing arms, but some early 1945/46 saloons mounted on 'spare' Kübelwagen chassis were fitted with gear reduction boxes on the outer ends of the driveshafts, giving better acceleration but a lower top speed. This arrangement was never intended for 'civilian' production.

1946

conditions. So tough and strong is the chassis, indeed, that a Beetle can be driven over rough roads as fast as it can on a smooth motorway and it is a credit to Dr Porsche's robust design that a good many older cars in existence today are still fitted with their original torsion springs.

Incidentally, not all chassis pans were fitted with jacking points in 1945. Those that were had round tubes into which the jack was inserted, but they proved unsatisfactory as cars often toppled off their jacks when raised off the ground, so square box-section fitments were introduced in 1946.

STEERING

Renowned for its precision and lightness, the steering is by transverse link and unequal length track rods. The steering box is a simple worm and nut affair which is clamped firmly to the upper torsion bar tube. A rubber bush is incorporated in the steering column to insulate the steering wheel against shocks transmitted through the road wheels. A lubrication nipple was incorporated into the inner tie rod but its position proved almost inaccessible to a standard size grease gun, so it was therefore suitably modified in 1946.

BRAKING

Until hydraulic brakes were introduced on the Export model in early 1950, the Beetle was fitted with cable-operated drum brakes on all four wheels. The four cables are enclosed in protective tubes and are operated under tension.

When the foot pedal is called into action, it forces the cable junction arm at the front of the chassis to move forward, thus pulling the cables at all four wheels. The handbrake operates on the same principle but is obviously not connected to the foot pedal shaft. Instead, it is attached via a ratchet to the handbrake linkage rod running through the backbone tunnel and operates on all four wheels.

The brake shoe assembly is entirely conventional and consists of a primary and a secondary shoe, two return springs, a shoe retainer spring on the top and bottom, shoe anchors and an operating lever. A clamping nut on the rear of the drums allows for shoe adjustments when the cables have stretched, which, with use, they most certainly will do.

The front drums are 230.1mm in diameter while those at the rear are 230mm. The front shoes were 30mm in width until October 1957 (chassis number 1-673410), when they were changed on the Export (but not the Standard) model for 40mm shoes. The width of the rear shoes remained at 30mm until 1968 (chassis number 118 328 505), when they were changed on the 1200, 1300 and 1500 models for 40mm shoes.

During 1946, production gathered at a healthy pace and, by October, the 10,000th car had been assembled despite continuing problems with the supply of raw materials. The factory had still to be fully repaired, workers had little food to eat and the Beetle was yet to be made available to the general public. It naturally follows that, crude as the VW was, precious little time or thought was given to improving the car at this stage.

Modifications, such as they were, included the fitment in the engine compartment of stiff cardboard, which had the effect of reducing engine noise in the cabin from an unbearable clatter to a slightly more acceptable rumble. An increase in tyre size from 4.50-16 to 5.00-16 was a 'tweak' which did little, if anything, to improve the roadholding.

Because of the immensely difficult working conditions at the Volkswagen factory, there were no improvements made to the interior of the Beetle. Materials were in short supply and seat fabrics, headlinings and interior panels did not become 'standardised' until the launch of the Export or de luxe model in 1949. Beetles emerging from Wolfsburg assembly lines between 1945 and 1949 were often and necessarily different in specification from one car to the next.

PRODUCTION CHANGES 1946

054 617
Pushrod tubes fitted with compressible corrugated ends instead of springs, but not on all cars.
057 390
Fuel tank located higher up.
058 568
Grease nipple of inner tie rod faced towards left rear wheel rather than rectangular to tie rod.
059 107
Grease nipple introduced on brake cables and tyres increased in size from 4.50-16 to 5.00-16.

Very few modifications were made during 1946 except that the majority of cars had been fitted with square jacking points by the end of the year.

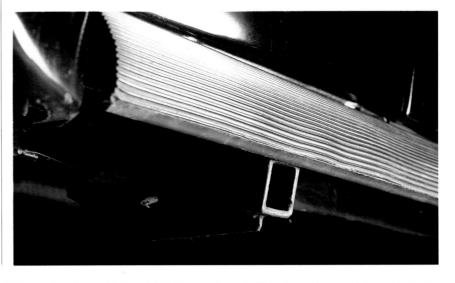

1947

In a year which saw the production of 8987 Beetles, the factory was still a pretty grim place but at last there was light at the end of the dark tunnel. Officially launched at the Hanover Fair, the Volkswagen was offered for sale to the general public despite the fact that few ordinary people could afford them. A batch of 56 cars was also exported to Holland, where Ben Pon became that country's official importer. It is significant that the cars he ordered were fitted with chromed hub caps and bumpers, for Beetles available on the home market still had painted items.

At around the same time, a number of Volkswagens found their way into Britain and the USA driven and imported privately by servicemen returning home after a long war. One such car owned by a Swedish gentleman was to fall into the hands of a highly respected Surrey-based car dealer, John Colborne-Baber, who took the Beetle in a part-exchange deal and drove it with such great enthusiasm that he decided to specialise in buying, selling and servicing Volkswagens and also offered a conversion to right-hand drive for UK customers. All the cars he bought and sold were secondhand, naturally, and weighed in at between £425 and £475 depending on the specification ordered.

Britain, like Germany in the immediate post-war years, was a pretty dreary place in many respects, so the Colborne Beetles were treated to high-quality resprays in bright gloss colours – the factory cars still had a matt finish. One Beetle manufactured on 12 August 1947, chassis number 68 380 and body number 17 287, was one of the first to arrive on British soil and, remarkably, is owned today by John Colborne-Baber's son, Peter, and registered JLT 420.

Resplendent in its famous two-tone blue paintwork, JLT has some 300,000 miles to its credit and, apart from a few details, is virtually as Peter's father intended it back in the late 1940s. Incidentally, Colborne Garages applied successfully to the Board of Trade for an import licence and became concessionaires for VW spares in 1950. A second import licence granted in 1952 enabled Colborne's to import Volkswagens (and Porsches) into Britain. Although an Irishman, Stephen O'Flaherty, founded Volkswagen Motors in 1953, the first official British dealership, John Colborne-Baber will always be thought of as the man responsible for introducing the Beetle to British shores.

JLT 420 occupies a special place in the hearts of everyday Volkswagen folk. Something of a 'hybrid', it has been restored in recent times and has been fitted with some non-original parts such as the bumpers and steering wheel, but, from a driving point of view, JLT is an excellent representation of what old man Porsche was getting at when he designed his People's car some 16 years earlier. Cable brakes, left-hand drive, a 'crash' gearbox, skinny

Thought to be the only remaining example of the many Beetles offered for sale in Britain during the late 1940s and early 1950s by the late John Colborne-Baber, this 1947 car is all the more interesting because it is owned today by Colborne's son, Peter. The Colborne Beetles differed from the normal factory cars in having gloss paintwork (two-tone if a customer preferred) and, in the case of JLT 420, bright trim applied to the running boards and bodywork.

crossply tyres, a roller throttle pedal, utterly appalling headlights and no more than 25bhp at your disposal all adds up to, in theory at least, a recipe for disaster on today's roads. Yet old JLT is an absolute delight, pulling 65mph on a motorway with ease, accelerating keenly when called upon to do so, and refusing to return less than 30mpg.

Exactly how many Beetles received a facelift in Colborne's hands is unclear, but JLT appears to be the only remaining example. But because these cars form an important part of the Beetle's history, you would be faced with a restoration dilemma were you to find one in the proverbial barn-fresh condition. In short, would you restore your Beetle to the original German specification or upgrade it to Colborne standards? Only the reader can make that decision.

One very minor bodywork alteration made in 1947 took the form of a steel bracket welded close to the brass chassis number plate on the apron under the bonnet into which security-conscious owners were encouraged to thread a sturdy chain to prevent thieves making off with the spare wheel. Also during this period, it is not unusual to find that some Beetles were fitted with just one windscreen wiper, on

Early cars are distinguished by attractive 'nipple' hub caps with a small V-over-W emblem in the centre, but were soon to be replaced, in 1948, by the more familiar domed items.

Leather seats and right-hand drive conversions were offered at extra cost on the Colborne-Baber Beetles, but this famous two-tone blue car was retained as left-hand drive.

Colborne Beetles were offered with seat fabrics and interior panels (blue leatherette in this case) that were more luxurious than those of the standard factory cars (right). The rear light pods (below) were always made in left-hand and right-hand pairs to take account of the curvature of the wings, but the lights themselves glow with less ferocity than a modern-day cigar lighter. Alloy bezels were introduced in 1946. The earliest of the post-war cars had the disadvantage that the heater knob (below right) was situated in the engine compartment, but it was moved, more conveniently, next to the handbrake lever in 1946. The choke button is situated close to the straight gear lever.

The turning bonnet handle (right) is correctly unchromed. The body number (far right) is stamped on the apron behind the spare wheel. Volkswagen would not have applied this bitumen protection.

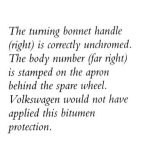

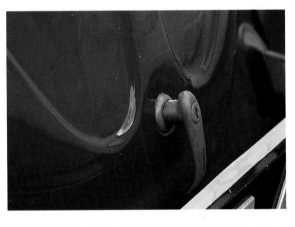

the driver's side, largely due to a shortage of materials in post-war Germany.

By now, it had become obvious to the Allies in the occupation zone that Germany's economic future was heavily dependent on exports. Beetles were displayed in showrooms throughout Germany during 1947 with a price tag of around 5000 Reichsmarks, and Dutchman Ben Pon took delivery of the first cars to be officially sold outside Germany. But it was not until the Hanover Fair, where the Beetle was launched to the public, that the car began to attract interest from foreign dealers. As the Beetle was still necessarily crude, it would be five years before Volkswagen could capitalise on the American market.

PRODUCTION CHANGES
1947

064 340
Reinforced ball bearings for rear hubs.
071 377
Bracket added for chain and lock to secure spare wheel.
071 616
For improved engine temperature control, fan housing fitted with manually adjustable flap which closes half of air-intake aperture to restrict air flow. Summer and winter setting.
073 348 (Oct)
Chassis number punched by stencil on tunnel between gear lever and handbrake lever.

With only 25bhp from the 1131cc flat-four engine, early Beetles were not fast, but this one, which has done over 300,000 miles, will easily pull 65mph. The chromed inlet manifold and pulley wheel are Colborne variations, as those fitted to the factory cars were painted.

This VDO speedometer (far left) is calibrated in miles per hour rather than kilometres, a Colborne modification for British customers. But the needle still runs 'backwards' like those fitted to the factory cars. The large bodywork aperture (left) is for a starting handle, a 'back-up' to the 6-volt electric starter on cold mornings.

1948

This 1948 car, owned by Hermann Walter, was one of the last of the standard Beetles, built just before the new Export model was introduced in 1949.

The impact made upon the Beetle's development after the appointment of ex-Opel general manager, Heinz Nordhoff, on 1 January 1948 can't be over-emphasised. A formidable man who commanded respect from everyone who worked at the factory, *Generaldirekteur* Nordhoff was the Beetle's most ardent critic in the early days. After all, the cars made between 1945 and 1949 were little altered from the pre-war prototypes. Apart from being noisy and devoid of creature comforts, they suffered from what today's marketing men would call an 'image problem'. Adolf Hitler had used the Beetle as an instrument of propaganda and although the

dictator had died in his bunker, 'his' car lived on.

For Nordhoff, cars like JLT 420 were simply not good enough, and he quickly concluded that if the Beetle was to succeed, particularly abroad, improvements would have to be made and made quickly. Nordhoff's appointment resulted in a turning point for the company because, by July 1949, the German manufacturer was poised for a major export drive with the announcement of the 'Export' or 'de luxe' model, a car which properly initiated Nordhoff's policy of continually improving the Beetle but never pandering to the whims of fashion. He even introduced a scheme whereby owners whose Beetles achieved the benchmark figure of 100,000kms with-out serious mechanical maladies would receive a commemorative watch and dashboard plaque, an interesting if expensive ploy which was continued until 1958.

The Beetle remained virtually unchanged through 1948 apart from a few very minor alterations. By May, the 25,000th car had been produced and, come January 1949, the Dutch importer, Ben Pon, had exported the first Beetle to the USA, where interest in the car proved less than encouraging.

PRODUCTION CHANGES 1948

090 690
Steering column with longitudinal groove for steering lock.

090 784
Modified brake drums; oil deflector and spacer widths increased from 12.9-13.1mm to 15.9-16.1mm.

Domed hub caps replaced the earlier 'nipple' items and the V-over-W emblem in the centre became much larger.

The spartan specification of the pre-Export cars meant that there was no exterior brightwork, even the door handles being painted (below).

1949

Production of the new Export or de luxe version began on 2 June with chassis number 1-106 636, and the model was officially launched to the public on 1 July. It was a much improved car, but the factory continued to offer the standard model for many years.

Two other important models appeared at roughly the same time: the four-seater cabriolet version produced by the Osnabrück-based coachbuilders Karmann from 3 June at the rate of one or two a day, and the Hebmüller two-seater cabriolet that first appeared at the German Motor Show in March. Unfortunately, the sought-after Hebmüller enjoyed an unfairly short production life. A factory fire on 23 July did not help matters, but these delectable motor cars were expensive and less practical than the Karmann four-seater. In 1952, Joseph Hebmüller and Son was declared bankrupt, having produced around 750 cars in total.

As one might expect, production changes on the Karmann cabriolets ran virtually parallel with the Export saloon, but inevitably these beautifully made 'ragtops' amounted to considerably more than 'tin-tops' with their roofs removed. Weighing some 200lb more than a saloon, the cabriolet was strengthened considerably with box-section girders. Because of the hood arrangement at the rear, air intake louvres for cooling the engine could not be employed in the same position, so they were instead cut vertically into the engine lid – but with the hood down these cars still tend to run hot when driven at high speeds for prolonged periods.

Since the cabriolets have enjoyed something of an exclusive cult status in recent times, their values have soared. In an attempt to cash in, a number of saloons have been converted by individuals and specialist companies who, in some instances, have not modified the bodywork to take account of the loss of structural strength inherent in removing the roof. Such cars can be considered at best worthless and at worst dangerous, and should be avoided at all costs.

Karmann cabriolets can be easily distinguished from home-made jobs. On a genuine car, the rear quarter panels and doors have a higher waistline, and the top of the windscreen frame is flatter. From the beginning, the right-hand front quarter panel was adorned with a rectangular 'Karmann Kabriolet' badge and, from July 1960, with a curved 'Karmann' badge. Non-genuine cars are not usually fitted with such elusive items. But more of the cabriolet later.

The Export saloon was the direct result of Nordhoff's pressing desire to improve the Volkswagen, for he realised early on that long-term success was almost solely dependent upon volume sales abroad and in no way could this be achieved with the agricultural cars of previous years. It is in the staggering attention to detail that the Export model can be distinguished from the standard car, and this eventually secured it a place at the top of the best-seller charts around the world.

Although the external dimensions remained the same, the Export version of the Volkswagen was treated to a major facelift which included synthetic gloss paintwork and a variety of colours. High quality alloy mouldings with a double-grooved contour were applied to the sides of the bodywork at waist level, to the centre of the bonnet and to the running boards. The headlamp rims, hub caps (now with a smaller VW emblem at their centres), door handles and bumpers were chromed. The bumpers were redesigned to include a central groove, and the rather gruesome overriders of the previous models were replaced by more rounded and less conspicuous chrome-plated items. With the introduction of gloss paint, the wheel rims were sprayed the same colour as the bodywork and the centres were usually (but not always) cream, a scheme which remained unaltered until the colours were reversed for the 1960 model year.

New curvaceous bumper overriders were a great improvement upon the earlier and gruesome 'sickle' type items. This chromed horn grille, seen on a 1951 car, is a 'dummy', placed on the right-hand side to balance the real one on the left. These grilles, introduced with the new Export model, were circular at first, but became oval in October 1952.

Large 16in diameter wheels with domed hub caps were retained until October 1952. They were usually painted with black rims and cream centres, a colour scheme that was reversed for the 1960 model year.

At the top of the bonnet, a VW emblem appeared for the first time and, at the bottom, a new pull handle replaced the turning variety as the bonnet release was now cable-operated from inside the car. The Bosch horn was repositioned on the underside of the left front wing (except on the standard model), with the result that the car gained a vent in the wing below the headlight to let out the sound. For the sake of neatness, this vent was fitted with a circular grille, while a matching dummy grille was added to the other wing to balance the frontal appearance.

On the engine lid, the registration plate pressing disappeared altogether, as did the hole for the starting handle with its bumper-mounted bracket and the previously lockable lid handle. A notable difference between the cabriolet and the saloon at this stage is the positioning of the semaphore indicators: on the cabriolet they were located in the front quarter panels, but moved in 1950 to the rear quarter panels just behind the doors.

Altogether more civilised than before, the Volkswagen's cabin was transformed from an inhospitable soundbox into something very much more snug and welcoming. Better soundproofing materials were employed in the engine compartment, the quality of the upholstery was improved considerably and the seats, now adjustable for rake, were typically covered in neatly-stitched cloth piped with vinyl. Instead of wing nuts for adjustment fore and aft, the Export car's seats were also fitted with spring-loaded handles from June, while the Standard car retained wing nuts

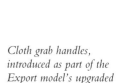

Grooved brightwork was applied to the bodywork and running boards of the Export model, but was replaced by 'smooth' trim in 1952. This design of pull-out door handle remained in use until 1959.

Cloth grab handles, introduced as part of the Export model's upgraded interior, were useful for rear seat passengers.

until the end of the 1965 model year, when it too gained the more modern items. Cushion rolls were even offered as optional extras to serve as armrests for rear passengers, but their ornate appearance was not to everyone's taste and they were discontinued at the end of 1951.

Also new for the Export model was a cream or

A far cry from the 'agricultural' cars of the early 1940s, post-Nordhoff Beetle interiors are stylish and comfortable, although the seats are typically firm. The optional cushion rolls for the rear seat are not fitted.

Export saloons were fitted with an ivory-coloured two-spoke steering wheel and matching control knobs, whereas those on the Standard car were in black. The presence of ventilation handles, one of which is just visible ahead of the passenger door, indicates that this is a 1951 car.

COLOURS

From July 1949
Black
Dark Red
Medium Brown
Pastel Green

These colours were current until April 1951

ivory coloured two-spoke steering wheel and a revised dashboard with bright trim. The control knobs on the dashboard, like the knobs for the window winders and gear lever, were colour-coordinated to match the steering wheel. To the right of the speedometer, a radio or clock (adjusted with a knob in the right-hand glovebox) could be more easily installed thanks to the inclusion of a removable Bakelite plate – fairly skilled handiwork with a hacksaw had been required to remove the previous sheet steel blanking plate. Whereas steel had previously been used for the glovebox linings, hard cardboard was employed in all cars made after May.

In the luggage compartment behind the rear seat, steel rails were embedded in the hard-wearing cord trim in order to offer greater support for heavy suitcases. The interior courtesy light was still at this stage mounted above the rear windows and operated by a switch on the windscreen wiper knob. The tunnel-mounted heater control pull knob, choke knob and horn button were ivory coloured, whereas those fitted to the standard cars were black.

The electrical system remained largely unchanged except that the fusebox was moved from its normal position next to the enlarged petrol tank and relocated on the left-hand inner front wing.

By this stage, the engine had come in for a number of small but nonetheless important changes generally aimed at improving longevity and reliability. The flat-topped air filter was substituted for one with a domed top in January, the vulnerable exhaust valves had their stems case-hardened from April, and the cylinder barrels were made with a higher phosphor content from September.

A number of modifications were made to the transmission throughout 1949. The majority need not detain us here, but by far the most significant was the transition from a magnesium-based alloy to elektron for the gearbox casing at the end of April. The casing was also redesigned to accept 2.5 litres of oil rather than the 3 litres used in the earlier cars.

It seems difficult to believe these days, but until October 1949 the throttle pedal was nothing more than a small circular roller. Instead of replacing it with a more conventional flat item, the factory merely increased its size – but this was at least an improvement. Purists argue, of course, that there was nothing wrong with the original item.

Earlier in the year, in April, the front suspension also came in for detail changes when the number of torsion springs in the lower axle tube was increased from four to five and those in the upper tube were

Introduced in 1949, the rails embedded in the rear luggage compartment lend extra support for heavy suitcases. The folding rear seat was a superbly practical feature.

reduced from five to four – in other words, a reversal of the previous arrangement. It was not until August that the single-acting telescopic shock absorbers in the front suspension were replaced by more modern double-acting units. However, both the cabriolet and saloon would have to wait until 1951 before the single-acting lever-type shock absorbers at the rear were similarly replaced by telescopic alternatives.

With the bonnet handle now fixed, the bonnet was opened by pulling an ivory-coloured knob under the dashboard. The knob remained, inconveniently, on the left on right-hand drive Beetles. Note the floor-hinged pedal layout and the enlarged throttle 'roller' introduced in October 1949.

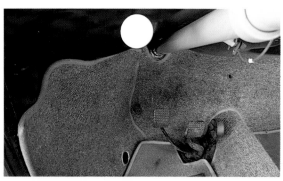

Double-acting telescopic shock absorbers were fitted to the Export model, at the front from 1949 and at the rear (seen here) from 1951.

PRODUCTION CHANGES 1949

092 918 (Jan)
Flat-topped air filter replaced by domed top.
094 554 (Feb)
Inlet manifold support introduced.
101 322 (Apr)
Front torsion spring numbers transposed: now five in lower tube and four in upper tube.
101 902 (Apr)
Exhaust valves receive case-hardened stems.
102 026 (Apr)
Elektron replaces magnesium-based alloy for gearbox casing.
1-0102 848 (May)
Fusebox relocated to inner left-hand front wing.
1-0106 717 (Jun)
Rear reflectors with anti-condensation protection.
1-0111 054 (Jul)
Pressing for number plate on engine lid dropped.
1-0116 375 (Aug)
Fuel tank shape modified, gauze strainer no longer fitted. Tank filler cap stamped with VW emblem.
1-0122 902 (Sep)
Higher phosphor content in cylinders.
1-0124 032 (Oct)
Brown rubber mats introduced in front footwells, sitting on rubber floorpan covering.
1-0126 157 (Oct)
Brake cables with Mipolam sheathing.
1-0128 058 (Oct)
Larger roller for throttle pedal.
1-0132 662 (Nov)
Shock absorbers now Boge or Hemscheidt, previously Hemscheidt only.

1950

In a year in which Nordhoff's efforts resulted in the production of the 100,000th Beetle, the car continued to be improved in an attempt to ensure that it would remain competitive both in Germany and in its still limited foreign markets.

Fresh air was very much a theme for 1950 with the introduction of small cut-outs in the tops of the door windows to allow ventilation of the cabin without the windows having to be completely opened. In addition, opening rear side windows and a sunshine roof were offered as optional extras. Today, opening side windows are rare as they were not considered, then as now, to be particularly desirable, but the beautifully made cloth sunroof most certainly was, and is. Manufactured by the specialist company of Golde and fitted at Wolfsburg by VW (from 28 April), the sunroof is more in the nature of a folding rather than a sliding panel, operating in tracks built into the roof panel. Secured at the front by a hook, the hard-wearing cloth material was squared off at all four corners to begin with, but became rounded off on the 1955 cars. Vinyl replaced cloth during 1956 and a more modern sliding steel sunroof was introduced in August 1963.

A number of changes were made to the 25bhp engine during the course of 1950. A large cylindrical air filter was substituted for the domed type of the previous year, a mechanical bellows-type thermostat was placed at the bottom of the engine in order to improve temperature regulation of the flat-four, and oil changing was made very much easier thanks to the inclusion of a drain plug in the strainer plate. Previously, the entire strainer plate had to be unbolted for the purpose of changing the oil. Engine noise inside the cabin was also reduced further after the introduction of additional sound-proofing encased in cylindrical tubes placed around the heater pipes under the rear seat.

Yet again, the front springing was altered with the result that the upper axle tube gained an additional torsion leaf in all cars built from January. With five torsion springs now in each of the two tubes, ride comfort was typically Germanic and firm, but, being manufactured to extremely high standards, the suspension was as unbreakable as ever.

Both the Export saloon and cabriolet versions were also treated to much-needed hydraulic brakes, and the master cylinder and fluid reservoir were installed below the petrol tank. The Beetle's hydraulic braking system is of an entirely conventional design and utilizes twin-shoe drums with a leading and trailing shoe for each drum. The front and rear drums are the same except that there is a linkage on the rear assembly for the handbrake. Naturally, the standard Beetle continued to be fitted with cable-operated brakes – the purist's choice.

This design of tail light remained in use until October 1952.

PRODUCTION CHANGES 1950

1-0138 835 (Jan)
Five torsion leaves in each torsion tube.
1-0140 243 (Jan)
Gaskets between cylinders and heads.
1-0155 020 (Mar)
Bosch headlights (previously of VW manufacture) introduced on saloon and cabriolet.
1-0156 129 (Mar)
Tailpipe increased in diameter from 31 to 32mm.
1-0156 970 (Apr)
Inlet manifold now made of light metal for improved pre-heating of mixture.
1-0156 991 (Apr)
Introduction of small cut-outs in tops of door windows.
1-0158 253 (Apr)
Hydraulic brakes introduced on Export saloon and cabriolet.
1-0161 234 (Apr)
Solex carburettor fitted with hinged float.
1-0162 580 (May)
Engine cooling regulated automatically by bellows thermostat to replace manually adjusted flap.
1-0167 890 (May)
Brake master cylinder reduced in size from 22.2mm to 19.5mm and rear wheel brake cylinders reduced from 19.05mm to 15.9mm.
1-0177 736 (Jul)
Carburettor fitted without hinged float from assembly numbers 213301 to 213455.

Before quarterlights were introduced in October 1952, draught-free ventilation after April 1950 was provided by a cut-out in the top of each door window glass. New cylindrical noise suppressors (below) covering the heater pipes, one on either side of the car beneath the rear seat, were extremely effective.

CHASSIS DATING	
Jan	144 319
Feb	149 883
Mar	156 683
Apr	162 448
May	169 063
Jun	176 987
Jul	182 236
Aug	189 755
Sep	197 738
Oct	205 956
Nov	213 957
Dec	220 133

1951

In what appeared at the time to be a workable solution to the perennial problem of providing fresh air ventilation, opening flaps were built in to the front quarter panels behind the wings on both the Export saloon and cabriolet versions.

As it turned out, they performed their function a little too well, blasting drivers and passengers alike with a constant stream of cold air at knee level. They were subsequently replaced for the 1952 model year by more controllable and user-friendly quarterlights in the door windows. The cut-outs in the top of the door windows continued until the advent of quarterlights. The ventilation flaps, which are operated by levers inside the car, are hinged at the rear and incorporate metal gauze to protect passengers from high-speed debris.

In all other respects, the bodywork remained unaltered except that bright trim appeared around the perimeter of the windscreen and was embedded firmly into the rubber seal, and a beautiful enamel badge was fixed to the bonnet between the polished aluminium handle and the central moulding. This badge, showing a reddish-brown wolf standing between the turrets of a white castle against a blue background, represents part of the coat of arms of the poor old Count of Schulenburg, on whose estate the Volkswagen factory was ordered to be built. Highly prized by collectors and vandals alike, the badges are easily removed and genuine replacements are rare. Happily, reproductions are available but tend to be expensive.

CHASSIS DATING	
Jan	228 324
Feb	235 856
Mar	242 698
Apr	248 875
May	255 651
Jun	263 981
Jul	272 486
Aug	281 220
Sep	289 399
Oct	298 569
Nov	307 652
Dec	313 829

As official exports to Britain did not get under way until 1952, this splendid 1951 car, owned by Paul Hough, is left-hand drive. The fresh air vents in the front quarter panels, just visible behind the front wing, were fitted only for 1951.

Although bright trim (left) was applied to the windscreen in 1951, it would be another year before the side and rear windows were similarly adorned. The spindly wiper arms were chrome-plated, but later painted silver. The VW badge at the top of the bonnet had arrived in 1949.

The opening flap of the fresh air vent (above) in each front quarter panel is operated by a handle inside the car. The gauze was intended to protect passengers from road debris. In practice, the vents worked too efficiently, creating a blast of cold air, and were discarded in 1952.

New optional extras to become available in 1951 included a dash-mounted grab handle and an additional perspex sun visor for the front passenger.

Right from the start of the year, the two crankcase halves were manufactured from elektron rather than magnesium-aluminium alloy and, from April, both the Export saloon and cabriolet were fitted at the rear with double-acting telescopic shock absorbers, which the front suspension gained in 1949.

A tinted perspex sun visor was standard on the driver's side, but became an optional extra for the passenger side in 1951.

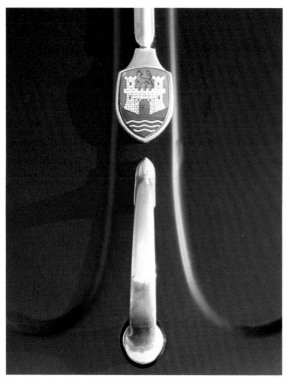

PRODUCTION CHANGES 1951

1-0221 638 (Jan)
Ventilation flaps fitted in front quarter panels.
1-0225 376 (Jan)
Crankcase made of elektron.
1-0243 731 (Apr)
Wolfsburg crest added to bonnet.
1-0244 003 (Apr)
Telescopic shock absorbers replace lever type on rear of Export saloon and cabriolet.
1-0244 668 (Apr)
Bright trim insert in windscreen rubber seal.
1-0253 756 (May)
Starter cable lengthened by 100mm, leading downwards from the side of the battery cover (previously leading towards the rear).
1-0272 706 (Aug)
Oil filler cap with clamp spring.
1-0287 416 (Sep)
Wheel bolts no longer included in tool kit.
1-0299 992 (Nov)
Tie rods with angular grease nipples (previously straight).
1-0304 210 (Nov)
Optional rear seat bolster cushions discontinued.

Depicting part of the Count of Schulenburg's coat of arms, the beautiful enamel badge showing Wolfsburg Castle first appeared in 1951. This style of polished aluminium bonnet handle had arrived in 1949.

COLOURS

From April 1951
Black
Azure Blue
Chestnut Brown
Pastel Green
Sand Grey

These colours were current until March 1953

1952

Up to and including 1952, the Beetle was modified, little by little, to the point where almost each one of its components (around 5000 in all) had been redesigned in some way or other. Porsche's basic concept remained, of course, but by this time the car was well-proven, reliable in every way, and able to compete with more conventional saloons from other manufacturers. In October 1952, however, came a cascade of changes which, in effect, produced the first of the Beetle's many annual facelifts.

The 1952 Export cars can be distinguished from those of the previous year by the bright bodywork trim which was 'smoothed out' rather than being grooved, and by additional brightwork fitted to the side and rear windows. After October, both doors had opening quarterlights installed, with the result that the window cut-outs were discontinued after just two years in use.

Also for 1952, both the horn grille on the left-hand wing and the dummy one on the right-hand side were modified, the round ones being replaced by oval units. At the rear of the car, the top of each

light pod was fitted with a lens which also served as a brake light, so the old Pope's nose was replaced by a number plate light pod more along the lines of the top half of a Dodo's bill, with a slight ridge down the middle. The engine lid handle became T-shaped, while the windscreen wiper arms were still the spindly wire type.

By far the most visible modification was the completely modified dashboard which, although not to everyone's taste, was an improvement over the old one. The new dash was introduced in October and despite the fact that it is more usually associated with the oval-window Beetles which appeared in March 1953, the last of the split-window cars were the first Beetles to be thus equipped.

Confronting the driver is a speedometer incorporating warning lights in red for the ignition system, green for oil pressure, blue for the headlight main beam and twin arrows pointing left and right for the indicators, which are operated by a stalk on the left of the steering column instead of by a switch in the middle of the dashboard. To the left of the speedometer is the starter button and lower down is

Although the Beetle looked much the same as ever, the last version of the 'Split' had been modified to the point where it had become a significantly different car from its predecessors. Spot lights, mud flaps, door mirrors, radio aerial and roof rack are all period accessories.

the ignition switch, to the right of the pull-out choke knob. Pull knobs located between the radio and steering column also operate the lights and windscreen wipers. In the centre is a space for the installation of a radio, above which a decorative grille conceals the speaker unit. A large pull-out ashtray is situated between the speaker and the single glovebox whose lid, which doubles conveniently as a tea tray, is opened with a push button.

The two-spoke steering wheel remained intact, but the ivory coloured central horn button was replaced with one featuring an attractive gold-on-black Wolfsburg Castle emblem surrounded by a chrome ring. Other interior modifications included a new style of heater rotary control knob offering greater scope for temperature adjustment than the old pull type, and a new location above the left-hand 'B' post for the interior light.

From October, a Solex 28 PCI carburettor replaced the 26 VFIS and was fitted with an accelerator pump and accelerator pump jet, which regulated the flow of the mixture more evenly and was responsible for eradicating the 'flat spots' so often suffered by the owners of previous models.

October was a popular month for changes, as this was when the front suspension torsion bars gained an additional leaf in each axle tube, making a total of six

in each. The gearbox gained cone-type synchromesh on second, third and fourth gears, but the standard Beetle continued with the more conventional 'crash' gearbox. Gear ratios on the Export version were as follows: first, 1:3.60; second, 1:1.88; third, 1:1.22; fourth, 1:0.79; reverse, 1:4.63. Gear ratios on the standard model were as follows: first, 1:3.60; second, 1:2.07; third, 1:1.25; fourth, 1:0.80; reverse, 1:6.60. At the same time the diameter of the five-stud wheels was reduced from 16in to 15in and they were shod with 5.60-15 crossply tyres.

The first German-built right-hand drive Beetle arrived on British soil at Dover on 7 April, having been assembled at Wolfsburg on 11 February. It was registered MRT 308 and took to the road on 9 April in the name of Miss Muriel Edwards. Although an assembly plant in Dublin had been churning out right-hand drive Beetles from 1950 and Colborne-Baber had offered a conversion on secondhand cars

Manufactured in January 1953, Dave Cantle's immaculate car includes all of the sweeping changes made in October of the previous year, including bright trim around the side and rear windows, separate lenses for the brake lights, quarterlights in the door windows, a modified version of the Pope's nose, revised bumpers and smoother bright trim on the bodywork and running boards.

Behind the spare wheel and above the body number stamped into the front apron is a plate giving details of various weights.

The brake lights (far left) were installed in the tops of the light pods in October 1952, but the skywards-angled lenses were obviously barely visible to following traffic. This is just one feature that highlights the potential dangers of driving an early 1950s Beetle in modern traffic. Both horn grilles at the front were modified in shape in October 1952, from circular to oval (left).

Introduced in October 1952, the new dashboard is more usually associated with the 'Oval' Beetles that appeared in March 1953. Much neater than before, it has a single glovebox with a lid, the radio speaker sits in the middle, and an ashtray is sited between the two.

The horn button gained a gold-on-black Wolfsburg Castle emblem in October 1952, and the starter button was moved to the left of the speedometer. The badge to the left of the starter button was awarded to all Volkswagen owners whose cars completed 100,000km trouble-free, a novel practice discontinued in 1958.

CHASSIS DATING	
Jan	322 798
Feb	331 318
Mar	339 822
Apr	348 714
May	358 632
Jun	368 640
Jul	375 154
Aug	385 990
Sep	397 014
Oct	408 537
Nov	418 301
Dec	428 156

By this stage, the glovebox lining was made of cardboard rather than steel, and the lid conveniently doubled as a tea tray. The new ashtray can also be seen.

for some time, MRT 308 was the first of the Wolfsburg-manufactured cars and survives to this day, now beautifully restored in the hands of Volkswagen connoisseur Frederick Metson in Northern Ireland. Incidentally, during 1953, when sales in Britain got under way, 945 cars were officially imported and all of them were 'ovals'.

PRODUCTION CHANGES
1952

1-0325 474 (Feb)
First factory-built right-hand drive Beetle, destined for UK market.
1-0357 667 (May)
One valve spring replaces two used previously.
1-0397 023 (Oct)
Significant bodywork and interior modifications, as described in text; intake manifold fitted with pre-heating tube in cast alloy jacket; synchromesh on 2nd, 3rd and 4th gears for Export model; six-leaf torsion springs in each front axle tube; shock absorber travel increased from 90 to 130mm; rear brake cylinders increased from 15.9mm to 17.5mm; fusebox for stop and tail lights placed on rear side of instrument panel instead of in the engine compartment as previously; Solex 28 PCI replaces 26 VFIS; 4J-15in wheels introduced with 5.60-15 tyres.

High quality cloth headlining offered passengers a feeling of cosiness. The courtesy light was moved from its former position above the rear windows to the left-hand side of the roof above the 'B' post.

The new style of rotary heater knob behind the handbrake lever was stamped with directional arrows.

From October 1952, a Solex 28 PCI carburettor replaced the 26 VFIS used previously. The new unit was fitted with an accelerator pump and regulated the flow of the mixture more evenly. Otherwise the engine remained unaltered, but the gearbox on the Export model gained synchromesh on the top three ratios.

1953

A small and newly-introduced chrome-plated push-button made it easier to open the quarterlights.

After 10 March 1953, the bodywork remained the same except that a one-piece oval window – which increased rear visibility by nearly 25 per cent – replaced the two-piece split design. The rear lights and registration light were unaltered and, significantly, there is still only a single tail pipe on the right-hand side.

As good as the Beetle undoubtedly was by 1953, Volkswagen's engineers and designers were nonetheless kept extremely busy in an attempt to improve the car further. By this time, there were important export markets to consider, including North America and Britain. Although the little car could not compete with the outrageously finned and chrome-encrusted gas-guzzlers popular in the US, the Volkswagen's appeal lay with its simplicity, economy, modesty and virtually unrivalled build quality.

For the restorer, 1953 is an especially important year because all the bodyshells made after 10 March had a one-piece oval rear window in place of the old split window, which had been a prominent feature since the production of the pre-war prototypes. The new window, which improved rearward vision considerably, continued up to 1957.

Because of the obvious advantages of the larger oval window, some Beetles made prior to 10 March had their split windows removed, the division being unceremoniously hacked out and the updated glass installed. With the benefit of hindsight, such a drastic course of action seems monstrous, but was carried out, quite understandably, in the name of safety. If your 'Split' has been 'Ovalled', you are faced with

the difficult decision of leaving it as it is or fabricating a new split window, a task not to be undertaken lightly. Incidentally, the new oval window was treated to bright trim from the outset, although cars converted to the Cal-look in recent times have almost universally had all the window trim removed – and finding replacements is not easy.

Interior changes were few: the quarterlights were fitted with push buttons, the dash-mounted smoker's companion gained a small chrome-plated handle, and the door striker plates on both the saloon and cabriolet became adjustable.

Naturally, the factory could not resist playing around with the front torsion bars and promptly increased the number of leaves from six to eight, again in the interest of improving ride comfort. The size of the petrol filler neck was increased from 40mm to 80mm on 10 March.

Between March 1953 and July 1957, there would be few external features to distinguish one model year from the next.

PRODUCTION CHANGES
1953

1-0433 397 (Jan)
Carburettor air correction jet 200 (previously 190).

1-0441 708 (Feb)
Door striker plate becomes adjustable.

1-0451 313 (Mar)
Tightening torque for cylinder head nuts now 3.6-3.8 mkg (previously 3 mkg).

1-0454 951 (Mar)
Oval rear window introduced (without central rib and 23% larger); ashtray receives handle; fuel filler neck enlarged to 80mm diameter.

1-0494 340 (Jun)
Solex 28 PCI ball valves made of bronze (previously steel).

1-0517 304 (Aug)
Front torsion bars increased from six to eight leaves.

1-0548 440 (Oct)
Rear suspension spring plate elongated by 2mm.

1-0551 808 (Nov)
Thickness of road wheel metal increased from 2.75mm to 3mm.

1-0562 054 (Nov)
Steering wheel design changed so that two spokes turn upwards, giving better view of speedometer.

1-0575 415 (Dec)
1131cc 25bhp engine discontinued and replaced by 1192cc 30bhp engine from 21 December; oil bath air cleaner standard for all Beetles; brake fluid reservoir behind spare wheel instead of at master cylinder.

1-0575 417 (Dec)
Dynamo uprated from 130W to 160W on all Beetles; ignition distributor fitted with vacuum adjustment; windscreen wipers now have flat-section arms, herringbone-section blades and arms now painted metallic grey/silver (previously chromed); fan belt made narrower with synthetic fibre inserts instead of rubber cord.

Excellent under-bonnet view shows the revised petrol filler neck, which was enlarged to 80mm diameter.

Leatherette seats are typical of the period, as is the chrome strip on the side panel. Note that rear seat passengers also have an ashtray built into the panel.

For right-hand drive cars, the dashboard was a reversal of those fitted to left-hookers, but in 1953 the ashtray gained a small handle.

From this angle, early 'Ovals' are virtually indistinguishable from late 'Splits'. Owned by John Maxwell, this car was manufactured in July 1953 and is one of just 945 examples sold in Britain that year.

Up to this time, the 1131cc engine was equipped with a variety of different shaped air cleaners. Containing a small quantity of oil to filter out foreign bodies, this 1953 oil bath version has a simple domed top.

COLOURS

From March 1953
Black
Pastel Green
Chestnut Brown
Atlantic Green
Sahara Beige
Metal Blue

These colours were current until January 1954

A T-shaped engine lid handle replaced the earlier vertical variety, while the registration light pod, also part of the October 1952 update, was now more along the lines of a Dodo's bill and slightly ridged in the middle.

1954

Several important modifications took place for the 1954 model year, although many of the alterations associated with the 1954 cars were actually instigated and fitted in December 1953.

Naturally, the bodywork remained unaltered, except that the rear light pods on North American cars were enlarged to make way for double-filament bulbs so that the stop and tail lights were housed behind one reflector, instead of having a separate and barely visible reflector on top of the housing as previously. However, non-US markets did not receive this important modification until l955. The short windscreen wipers, also altered at the end of 1953, became flat rather than rounded, had herringbone-section blades, and the arms were painted a grey/silver colour instead of being chromed.

Inside the car, the seats were more comfortable as better quality fabrics became available and the rear seat was secured with a rubber strap to prevent it slamming down under very heavy braking. Now fitted into the left-hand side of the roof and close to the door, the interior courtesy light was wired to a switch which automatically turned the bulb on and off when the doors were opened and closed.

The dashboard-mounted starter button was dropped altogether, and replaced by a key-operated switch on the dashboard. Located beneath the ashtray some distance from the driver, the new ignition key provided endless amusement for young children, who often discovered that they could cause mischief by switching off the engine at will, by turning the key one notch to the left. It would be a good many years before Volkswagen saw fit to put the key out of

CHASSIS DATING	
Jan	594 689
Feb	609 909
Mar	627 474
Apr	643 364
May	660 135
Jun	676 878
Jul	687 170
Aug	703 464
Sep	722 716
Oct	742 329
Nov	761 706
Dec	781 884

Production of the Karmann four-seater cabriolet began in June 1949 and its development ran roughly parallel to its 'tin-top' sister. Made in 1954 and owned by Howard Chadwick, this car differs most visibly from the pre-1951 cabriolets in that its semaphore indicators are embedded in the rear quarter panels rather than in the front inner wings. Irrespective of age, cabriolets had a one-piece glass rear window. With the hood down, the styling closely resembles many pre-war Mercedes-Benz cabriolets.

harm's way on the steering column.

During this period, the rubber foot pads fitted to the clutch and brake pedals displayed the VW emblem at their centres, but don't expect them to last very long if you drive your car regularly. They have a tendency to wear out quickly, particularly the variety available for just a few pence at Volkswagen shows. The heater vents in the front footwells were now covered with wire gauze; they had bright metal surrounds and they were larger than before. The ivory-coloured heater control knob was no longer marked with arrows to show the direction of rotation.

Until this time, much of the work done to improve the Beetle was aimed principally at bodywork adornment, creature comforts, ergonomics and the like, but the faithful 25bhp 1131cc engine had remained virtually unaltered. So the decision was taken to increase the flat-four's size to 1192cc. The compression ratio was raised at the same time from 5.8:1 to 6.1:1 initially (December 1953), and later to 6.6:1 (August 1954). The engine's power output, as a result, took a comparatively massive leap from 25bhp to 30bhp, produced at 3400rpm. The four inlet valves were increased in diameter from 28.6mm to 30mm, to improve breathing, and the distributor gained a vacuum advance mechanism.

In today's motor cars, a 5bhp increase would hardly be noticeable even by a more sporting driver, but until 21 December 1953, when the new power unit was installed, the Beetle was underpowered even by the standards of its contemporaries. The larger-engined cars, therefore, were welcomed with open arms even by those who harboured little or no desire to reach the dizzy heights of 60mph plus. In its 1954 Beetle road test, *The Autocar* recorded a top speed of 62.5mph and 0-50mph in 22.2sec, a gain of 0.7sec over the old 25bhp car despite the inevitable weight penalty of the Beetle's year-on-year modifications.

It is interesting that performance figures quoted by Volkswagen and independent sources throughout the car's production life were often at variance with those claimed by the people who actually owned and drove Beetles. Most manufacturers, including Volkswagen, have produced their own versions of the dreaded 'Monday morning' car, which would not go if it was attached to a Vulcan bomber. But every now and then there were the 'Wednesday afternoon' Beetles whose performance far exceeded what could normally be expected from such a humble and understressed power unit. If you have a Beetle that appears to want to charge on to 75mph in third gear and 90mph in top, and there are some that do, then make sure you look after it!

Conveniently, the brake fluid reservoir was moved to the well in the front apron behind the spare wheel and had a screw top – previously it had been inaccessibly fitted under the petrol tank in tandem with the brake master cylinder.

TECHNICAL OUTLINE

1192cc 30bhp
Capacity 1192cc
Bore and stroke 77×64mm
Compression ratio 6.6:1
Max power 30bhp at 3400rpm
Gear ratios
1st   3.60:1
2nd   1.88:1
3rd   1.23:1
4th   0.82:1
Reverse 4.63:1
Final drive ratio 4.375:1

Luxury fresh-air motoring for those who could afford it. Genuine cabriolets can be distinguished from 'home-made' conversions by the curvaceous panelwork above the waistline bright trim. Note the semaphore indicator in the rear panel behind the door and the more comfortable seating introduced for the 1954 model year. This car has a number of period extras, including the steering wheel (usually found on low-volume coachbuilt Volkswagens) and additional instrumentation in the centre.

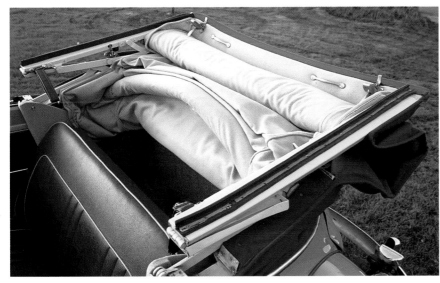

For the greater part of the cabriolet's production life, the hood (above) was made with a vinyl exterior, a plastic headlining and a heavy horsehair and rubber filling. Enlarged heater vents (right) with bright metal surrounds and wire gauze covers appeared in 1954, while the clutch and brake pedal rubbers displayed the VW emblem. The roller ball throttle pedal soldiered on until a more conventional flat pedal replaced it for the 1958 model year.

PRODUCTION CHANGES 1954

1-0599 151 (Feb)
Gearbox synchroniser stop ring modified in shape.

1-0611 493 (Mar)
Petrol tank filler cap galvanised inside and outside with hydronalium.

1-0623 266 (Mar)
Diameter of front and rear brake hoses increased from 10mm to 12.2mm.

1-0631 062 (Apr)
Dimensions of oil pump housing modified to clear oil pump shaft.

1-0645 501 (May)
Wheel brake cylinders awarded four mounting bolts instead of two.

1-0696 501 (Aug)
Spare fan belt no longer supplied in tool kit.

1-0702 742 (Aug)
Compression ratio raised to 6.6:1; 28 PCI carburettor, main jet 117.5 and air correction jet 195 (previously 122.5/200).

1-0722 916 (Oct)
Stop light window on rear light pods discontinued on US cars.

1-0734 000 (Oct)
Rear light pods fitted with water drainage aperture.

1-0753 096 (Nov)
Fan wheel and small pulley dynamically balanced.

Introduced in December 1953, the more powerful 30bhp 1192cc engine is visually indistinguishable from the 25bhp 1131cc unit it replaced, but owners welcomed the power increase with open arms.

The master cylinder brake fluid reservoir, with a screw top, was positioned in the front apron well in 1954.

COLOURS

From January 1954
Black
Strato Silver
Light Blue
Metallic Brown
Iceland Green

These colours were current until August 1955

1955

'Ovals' are among the most desirable of all Beetles because of their looks and exceptional build quality. Although this Belgian-built car, owned by Nick Carr-Forster, was manufactured in October 1956, it actually follows the previous 1956 model year specification introduced in August 1955.

With the Beetle now in its 10th year of production since the end of the war, Volkswagen not only celebrated its one millionth Beetle on 5 August but also came to symbolise the new German economic miracle, as a model example by which the success of all other companies would be measured. Still under Nordhoff, whose faith in the Beetle remained unshakeable, the factory continued to modify and refine what was basically a 24-year-old design while other manufacturers throughout Europe and North America launched wholly new models. This year, 1955, also marks the start of the August-to-August model year system, whereby significant production changes occurred after the traditional factory shutdown.

While customers in North America were treated

to new double-filament stop and tail lights in 1954, Beetle buyers in the rest of the world had to wait until 1955. Export cars bound for North America in 1955 also had the added advantage of flashing direction indicators with clear lenses built into the sides of the front wings whereas European cars retained semaphores for another five years. Incidentally, the revised tail lights were repositioned higher up on the rear wings, a change that not only made them more visible to the drivers of following cars but also improved the Beetle aesthetically – this small point is not easy to spot but noteworthy just the same.

Beetles destined for North America were also fitted with special reinforced bumpers with taller overriders and an additional bar above the existing blades to offer further bodywork protection in a country

whose cities were already becoming overpopulated with cars. Many Beetles equipped with these American-spec bumpers found their way into other countries, including Britain, but nowadays these heavy-duty items, much sought after by restorers in Europe, are becoming increasingly difficult to find in good condition. Those fitted to unrestored cars will have almost certainly become tarnished and pitted with rust spots by now, so the only sensible route to rectify corrosion damage is to seek the services of a rechroming specialist. Since there is a lot more metal in the 'American' items, a worthwhile job will tend to be more expensive.

Under the bonnet, the fuel tank was reshaped with a flatter top and a deeper bottom in order to increase luggage space, and the size of the filler neck was

reduced from 80mm to 60mm. The heavy jack, so strong that it is capable of lifting one side of the car at a time, was secured by a steel clip in the well to the right of the spare wheel. With older unrestored Beetles, it is not recommended that the genuine jack is used for changing a wheel unless the car's sills are known to be in good condition, because the former has a nasty habit of embedding itself in the latter. As a result, the Beetle has a quite unjust reputation for weak jacking points, although it is seldom the case that the actual jacking points go so rusty that they can't be used. The real problem area is the rear part of the sills, which can corrode so badly that the jack not only breaks the sill but often damages the quarter panel as well.

Whereas the standard model continued to be fitted

Not a flat surface or a sharp edge in sight. It is not difficult to see from this angle why the air-cooled Volkswagen gained its Beetle nickname.

COLOURS

From August 1955
Polar Silver
Strato Silver
Black
Jungle Green
Rush Green
Nile Beige

with a three-spoke steering wheel and black plastic operating knobs on the dashboard, the Export car received a slightly modified version of the two-spoke wheel with a smaller hub and deeper spokes. The front seats were also updated, becoming some 30mm wider and having backrests that were adjustable to three different positions by turning a metal knob situated at the base of the framework. At the same time, the Export Beetle was fitted with attractive vinyl and cloth door panels matched by similar panels in the rear. To prevent the doors opening further than their hinges would naturally allow, they were fitted with strong metal stays to replace the cloth straps which had a tendency to stretch in use.

Because the heater control knob was located further forward on the tunnel for easier use by the driver, the gearlever was cranked in the centre. To help prevent car theft, the small handle for opening the quarterlights was redesigned with a more curved shape and was better seated, so as to make it more difficult to open in the event of some sad character prising open the window with a screwdriver.

Although many accessories were available for the Beetle by this stage, some are considerably less useful than others. Particularly popular items which have enjoyed something of a revival in recent times are the 'eyelids' which fit over the top of the headlights, but, cute as they may look to some, they create considerable drag and reduce top speed by 5-10mph. A flower vase for the dashboard, however, is a 'must', if a slightly expensive one these days.

From August 1955, the exhaust system was modified with a single chamber tailbox with a connecting pipe for improved induction pre-heating, and the use on Export cars of two chrome-plated tailpipes instead of a single pipe. One extremely useful modification beneath the engine lid from August was the reduction in size of the dynamo pulley nut from 36mm to 21mm, which allows the same tool to be used for changing the fan belt and the spark plugs.

PRODUCTION CHANGES
1955

1-0787 449 (Jan)
Tie rods without grease nipples for 1000 Standard saloons, up to chassis number 1-0797 357.

1-0805 122 (Feb)
Reinforced outer ring for horn button housing.

1-0929 746 (Aug)
Significant bodywork and interior modifications, as described in text; spark plug spanner now fits 21mm dynamo pulley nut; single chamber exhaust box with two tailpipes (chromed on Export model, painted black on Standard) and connecting pipe for pre-heating tube; steering gear limited by lateral stops at upper axle tube; steering wheel on Export model modified in shape with spokes arranged lower; heater knob moved forward and gear lever cranked; handbrake cables attached to handbrake lever on Export cars instead of being attached to brake rod; shape of fuel tank modified, filler neck reduced in diameter to 60mm; quarterlight handles redesigned in interests of security.

CHASSIS DATING	
Jan	802 662
Feb	823 604
Mar	847 966
Apr	869 399
May	892 300
Jun	916 456
Jul	929 512
Aug	953 486
Sep	981 573
Oct	1008 157
Nov	1034 731
Dec	1060 929

Instead of being mounted in the top of the tail light pods, the brake lights were incorporated into the tail lights, where they were more easily visible.

The V-over-W emblem in the centre of the hub caps (left) was sometimes highlighted in a colour until September 1956, but black was always used by the factory thereafter.

While European and British cars soldiered on until 1960 with semaphore indicators (right), Beetles exported to North America gained more modern wing-mounted flashing indicators from 1955.

The 'easy-grip' steering wheel, introduced in 1955, had deeper-set spokes to allow an easier view of the speedometer. The dashboard remained unchanged, but the doors now had new vinyl/cloth trims and the front seats were 30mm wider.

Mounted on the right-hand of the spare wheel, the jack (right) is so strong that it can easily lift the whole side of a Beetle, although it's advisable to check sill condition before trying this. After August 1955, the heater control knob (far right) was moved further forward on the backbone tunnel and, consequently, the gear lever was cranked rather than straight.

1956

Through a year in which the Suez oil crisis threatened doom and gloom for motoring folk in general, production continued at Wolfsburg at unabated pace and, surprisingly, the Beetle remained virtually unaltered from the previous year. But changes were made nonetheless, even if it takes a real expert to spot them.

There were no bodywork modifications as such, but the cabriolet's steel hood studs were replaced by corrosion-resistant brass items. From early September, the VW emblem in the centre of the hubcaps was always highlighted in black, whereas previously a variety of colours had been available. Considered to be something rather special at the time, an experimental batch of 800 cars built in June were fitted with 5.60-15 tubeless tyres, which became standard on 10 July. It would be another four years before the English rally driver, Bill Bengry, had the opportunity to go rallying in a Beetle fitted with Pirelli Cintura radials for the first time. In March, the ground clearance of the Export model was reduced from 172mm to 155mm.

Engine modifications for this otherwise comparatively barren year included a change from Resitex material to aluminium alloy for the camshaft timing gear. Early Beetles, including the one owned in the mid-1950s by Bill Boddy, editor of *Motor Sport*, had a tendency to strip their timing gears. Having been inconvenienced by this perennial malady, Boddy continued to drive a Beetle with extraordinary enthusiasm for many years, promoting its virtues and apparently viceless character in his esteemed journal whenever the opportunity presented itself.

There are always exceptions to any rule, but the cars produced by Volkswagen from 1954 to the end of 1958 – and particularly those in 1956 – are among the very best in the Beetle's history in terms of build quality and engineering excellence. Many Beetles manufactured at this time remain in sparkling condition, having never been restored by loving owners who often go to quite extraordinary lengths to preserve their steeds in first-class order.

It is often the case that the paintwork retains its remarkably deep shine, the doors still close with a heavy 'clunk', and there is an overall feeling of the kind of solidity only found in expensive luxury saloons from Daimler-Benz and Rolls-Royce. It is surely sufficient testimony to the Beetle's engineering integrity that a former chief engineer at Rolls-Royce, Harry Grylls, who was responsible for the Silver Shadow, bought a Beetle for his retirement in the late 1960s.

CHASSIS DATING	
Jan	1089 519
Feb	1117 569
Mar	1146 396
Apr	1173 573
May	1201 428
Jun	1231 530
Jul	1246 318
Aug	1276 742
Sep	1305 700
Oct	1338 159
Nov	1368 326
Dec	1394 119

Simon Parkinson's father bought this Beetle new in April 1957 and clocked up more than 70,000 miles before he sold it in 1965. Nine years later, the Parkinsons bought it back and restored it. The white-wall tyres were particularly popular with American customers.

The 30bhp engine had remained virtually unaltered since it was introduced in December 1953, but better sound-proofing material was employed in the compartment from 1956.

In contrast to the Beetle illustrated in the previous model year, this car (above) has red leatherette upholstery, which is much easier to keep clean. The luggage space behind the rear seat (right) can swallow large suitcases, as with this period set that was specially designed to fit the compartment.

PRODUCTION CHANGES
1956

1 084 218 (Jan)
Draught seal at carbon bush in steering column tube with rubber washer.

1 165 108 (Apr)
Distance from centre of petrol tank to centre of filler neck reduced from 245mm to 215mm.

1 210 230 (Jun)
Vacuum pipe now below throttle control cable (previously above air control cable).

1 227 367 (Jun)
Semaphore indicator arms become yellow with red shades on Inca Red cabriolet, yellow shade only from August.

1 232 835 (Jul)
Tubeless tyres fitted to 800 vehicles.

1 239 921 (Jul)
Tubeless tyres become standard.

1 243 559 (Jul)
Windscreen wiper motor fitted with 'permanent' magnet (SWF make) in 10,000 vehicles.

1 259 940 (Aug)
Bore for oil pump shaft increased in length from 23mm to 25mm.

1 266 678 (Aug)
Timing gear changes from Resitex to aluminium alloy.

1 304 254 (Sep)
Transmission oil SAE 80 specified for October to March, instead of SAE 90.

1 378 864 (Dec)
Clutch: new thrust spring cross section and clutch pressure reduced.

1957

After the traditional factory shutdown in August, a heavily revised Beetle was launched for the 1958 model year, paving the way for a new and altogether more modern era in which safety in particular was soon to become a more prominent issue. To that end, the factory at Wolfsburg waved goodbye to the last of the oval-windowed cars, chassis number 1-0 600439, at the end of July and launched the first of the 'big-window' Beetles.

Apart from replacing the oval glass with a rectangular window which nearly doubled rearward vision, the windscreen – still completely flat at this stage – was also enlarged, a modification achieved by slimming down the A-posts. Whereas 'Ovals' were snug and cosy, the latest offering was bright and airy. Not surprisingly, it was well received by Volkswagen's now exceptionally loyal clientele.

As a direct result of the increased size and altered shape of the rear window, the air-intake louvres for the engine cooling system became less shapely and were shortened considerably. At the same time, the engine lid was redesigned: although the result was pleasing enough, it was less conspicuous, less Beetle-like and much less stylish than the 'W' lids of yesteryear. The cabriolet, which until now had vertical air louvres cut into its engine lid, was modified with horizontal slots which arguably softened the styling for the better. Naturally, the cabriolet's windscreen and rear window were also enlarged. To improve

lighting at the rear, spherical bulbs replaced festoon bulbs for the stop, tail and number plate lights.

Yet again, the dashboard was completely redesigned; although ergonomically more satisfactory, it was less appealing aesthetically. In short, the 'cosy' factor had been removed to a certain extent, as had a small part of the Beetle's essential character.

The radio speaker was now placed behind a vertically-louvred grille to the left of the speedometer on left-hand-drive cars (to the right for right-hand-drive), while a second grille was sited on the other side of the speedometer for the sake of balance. On Export cars only, a bright moulding strip running horizontally through the centre of the grille was continued across the entire width of the dash panel. The radio was moved to the centre of the dash, higher up than previously. Since a radio was an optional extra, fitting one required the removal of a blanking plate, which was also trimmed with the new moulding. These modifications allowed for a usefully wider glovebox, but this meant that the rather attractive pull-out ashtray of the previous models had to be discarded in favour of a smaller sliding item. Mounted below the radio, it always managed to produce a fearful scraping noise when pulled out or pushed in. The control knobs for the lights and wipers moved to the top of the dash above the radio, while the ignition switch was positioned closer to the driver.

The door and rear side panels were refashioned in

The windscreen was enlarged (far left) by slimming down the A-posts and making the roof shorter at the front. Because the rear window had also been enlarged, the rear view mirror was increased in size. The increased size of the rear window (left) made the cabin brighter, and therefore a little less cosy.

The glovebox was enlarged considerably (far left), the light and windscreen wiper switches were better spaced, and the ashtray, which always makes a terrible scraping noise, was placed below the radio. For the first time since October 1952, the dashboard was completely modified (left). The radio speaker grilles were placed either side of the speedometer and, except on the Standard model, bright trim was added.

The 1958 model year saw the arrival of the first of the 'big window' cars, a move which brought the Beetle into the modern age. But semaphore indicators were retained, which is why this regularly-used car – from a year in which survivors are surprisingly rare – has been updated by owner Eva Miller with 'bolt-on' flashers. To accommodate the larger glass, the air louvres were shortened and the engine lid was modified.

COLOURS

From August 1957
Black
Coral Red
Diamond Grey
Light Bronze
Capri
Fern Blue
Agave

vinyl rather than a combination of cloth and vinyl as previously, and the driver was treated not only to a larger rear-view mirror but also to a more conventional flat rubber-covered accelerator pedal in place of the roller ball type.

From September 1957, the Beetle also became much quieter, at least from a passenger's point of view, with the introduction of additional sound-proofing material in the rear luggage bay and over the interior surfaces of the rear wheelarches. For restoration purposes, this sound-proofing can cause problems: although the heavy wool materials used are very effective at absorbing engine noise, they are equally good at retaining moisture, with the result that the underlying panels can rot badly.

At the 'business end', the 30bhp engine remained unchanged, but the oil bath air cleaner was modified in shape to become taller and smaller in diameter. The oil cooler was made shorter, and was now brazed instead of soldered.

By this time, Volkswagen of America had been established for just two years, but already Americans were completely sold on the idea of a noisy and cramped car that was almost unimaginably different from their chrome-encrusted V8s. By the time the famous deprecatory advertising campaigns began, the American public no longer needed convincing.

PRODUCTION CHANGES 1957

1 394 163 (Jan)
Heater outlets in front footwells moved back.

1 585 100 (Jul)
Oil cooler to a shorter design and brazed rather than soldered.

1 600 440 (Jul/Aug)
Significant bodywork and interior modifications, as described in text; windscreen and rear window enlarged; distance between wiper arms reduced; larger blades wipe larger area; registration light relocated at a higher level with light dispersion lens; oil bath air cleaner modified, higher but smaller in diameter; plastic bush in steering column 50 per cent smaller (previously synthetic with rubber casing); plastic foam layer between fuel tank and luggage compartment (previously cardboard); engine lid air intake louvres on the cabriolet horizontal, previously vertical.

1 649 253 (Sep)
Self-cancelling semaphore indicators introduced; additional sound-proofing for rear luggage bay and rear wheelarches.

1 676 789 (Oct)
Registration light bulb round instead of festoon type.

1 708 050 (Oct)
Brake and indicator light bulbs round instead of festoon type.

1958

1959

CHASSIS DATING

Jan	1815 645
Feb	1852 703
Mar	1891 481
Apr	1926 948
May	1962 835
Jun	2001 110
Jul	2020 302
Aug	2060 332
Sep	2102 988
Oct	2149 028
Nov	2186 987
Dec	2226 206

Through 1958 and 1959, there were relatively few modifications by Volkswagen's standards, Nordhoff continuing with the idea that change merely for the sake of it was pointless. Customers throughout the world obviously agreed with him because sales continued to soar.

Today, the cars made in this period are not as highly prized as 'Ovals' or 'Splits', but they are, nevertheless, of exceptional quality and have the added advantage of being inexpensive to buy. Spare parts are also more easily obtainable and again cost very little. If you don't feel like stretching your pocket to acquire and run one of the older cars, a '58 or a '59 may well be ideal.

The bodywork remained unchanged and mechanical alterations were confined largely to the gearbox, which gained a very useful magnetic oil drain plug that made an excellent job of gathering up and retaining metallic swarf. The Solex 28 PCI carburettor was fitted with a venturi tube made of nylon instead of alloy, and the spark plug spanner now came with a rubber insert to make servicing a good deal easier.

Among detail changes on the 'big-window' Beetle, the roller ball throttle pedal was at long last replaced by a more conventional flat pedal.

PRODUCTION CHANGES 1958

1 789 807 (Jan)
Oil drain plug in gearbox now magnetic.

1 802 775 (Jan)
Spring for idling screw on 28 PCI carburettor reduced from 13.5mm to 12mm.

1 832 100 (Feb)
Steering gains rubber seal ring at top in place of wax-dipped felt gasket.

1 882 550 (Mar)
Spark plug spanner fitted with rubber sleeve for easier use in servicing.

1 938 979 (May)
Kingpin thrust washer now white plastic, to replace fibre washer.

1 975 105 (Jun)
28 PCI carburettor fitted with nylon venturi instead of aluminium alloy.

COLOURS

From August 1958
Black
Fjord Blue
Diamond Grey
Capri
Carnet Red
Mignonette
Kalahari Beige
Jupiter Grey

The Beetle's appearance again remained largely unaltered, but under the skin there were important modifications that would be retained for the car's remaining production life.

The only distinguishing features changed on the outside of the car were new fixed door handles with rectangular push buttons and a new bonnet-mounted emblem depicting Wolfsburg Castle. The latter was redesigned to become, from August, less colourful and simpler, but today these items are just as desirable to the light-fingered brigade.

The Export model's steering wheel received a redesign: although the hub retained its attractive Wolfsburg crest, the two spokes were much more deeply dished and a semi-circular ring was added for operating the horn. Over the years, these horn rings have demonstrated a propensity for snapping (usually when you are not looking so that everyone who has been near the car in the past 10 years is suspected), but they can easily be replaced, or repaired and rechromed, if necessary.

Front seat passengers were treated to a footrest in the form of a piece of black-painted sheet steel set at a convenient angle, and also to a dished armrest to provide better grip when opening and closing the door. Although still typically firm, the front seats were softened and the backrests were more deeply curved to offer significantly better lateral support under hard cornering.

In the rear, plastic-covered inserts were installed to blank off the gaps under the rear seat between the backbone tunnel and the sills. Apart from tidying up the appearance of the interior, these went a long way to suppressing engine noise inside the cabin. Simple items whose significance is difficult to appreciate until they are removed, the boards make such a big difference that if you take them out while other restoration work is in progress, it is worth storing them away very carefully.

Further measures to reduce engine noise in the cabin included additional sound-proofing material on the horizontal panel that forms the floor of the luggage well behind the back seat, and bitumen felt applied to the two halves of the floorpan. The latter not only absorbs engine clatter but also damps down with extraordinary effect the racket from stone chippings hitting the underside of the chassis. However, if you are considering a complete restoration of your floorpan, which obviously necessitates the removal of the bitumen, it's not a bad idea to take yourself off to the pub for a couple of hours first – the job is extremely difficult and incomparably messy.

The really important changes in 1959 were made in the handling and roadholding departments. For many years the Beetle had received considerable, but not wholly justified, criticism for its inherent tendency to oversteer. A combination of rear weight bias, swing-axle suspension and narrow rear track

CHASSIS DATING

Jan	2 270 326
Feb	2 312 649
Mar	2 355 192
Apr	2 405 422
May	2 447 564
Jun	2 498 431
Jul	2 528 282
Aug	2 574 497
Sep	2 631 447
Oct	2 690 897
Nov	2 745 953
Dec	2 801 613

COLOURS

From August 1959
Black
Indian Red
Arctis
Flint Grey
Indigo Blue
Jade Green
Mango Green
Ceramic Green

The dashboard (above) was unchanged, but the two-spoke steering wheel was redesigned and a semi-circular horn rim was introduced.

Instead of the earlier pull-out style, the new 'safety' door handles (far left) were fixed in position and operated by pressing the rectangular button. Upholstered sun visors (left) replaced the attractive tinted perspex items.

From August 1959, the bonnet-mounted Wolfsburg crest (right) was simplified and became less colourful. In an effort to reduce sound levels in the cabin, heel boards were installed below the rear seat (far right) and bitumen felt was applied to the two halves of the floorpan.

1960

had sometimes caught out inexperienced drivers, so, true to form, Volkswagen's engineers went part way to silencing dissent by fitting an anti-roll bar at the front and, at the rear, lowering the pivot point of the swing axles by as much as 15mm by the simple expedient of tilting both the engine and gearbox forward by two degrees.

Both modifications had the effect of making the handling more neutral in normal driving conditions and more predictable on the limit. It is interesting that Bill Bengry, who won the RAC Rally Championship in both 1960 and 1961 driving Beetles, actually removed the front anti-roll bar from his competition cars, insisting that a tail-happy Beetle was quicker through corners.

From May, the connections between the heat exchangers, tailbox and tail pipes were fitted with conical asbestos seals and held in position with clips. From August, the 28 PCI carburettor was modified and the distributor was installed with vacuum advance only.

Thanks to the considerable efforts of Heinz Nordhoff, the Beetle had surpassed all sales expectations. More than 50,000 employees at Wolfsburg were building some 4000 cars per day, but their efforts were still not able to satisfy public demand. Dealers' waiting lists grew even longer, and in America there was even a black market for new Beetles…

PRODUCTION CHANGES 1959

2 245 160 (Jan)
Hub cap removal tool included in tool kit.

2 256 907 (Jan)
Tie rod modified on right-hand-drive cars, length of left tie rod reduced from 814mm to 807mm, length of right tie rod increased from 318mm to 325mm.

2 303 976 (Feb)
Distributor with vacuum spark timing advance only and carburettor with additional drilling in lower part of body (5000 engines intermittently).

2 409 056 (May)
Modified heater junction box.

2 425 182 (May)
Connection between exhaust boxes, tailbox and tail pipes fitted with conical asbestos seals and secured with clips.

2 528 668 (Aug)
Minor bodywork and interior modifications, as described in text; steering wheel fitted with semi-circular horn rim; ratio of crankshaft pulley/fan drive 1:1.75 (previously 1:2); distance from tip of oil dipstick to upper oil level marking reduced to 40mm from 44mm; anti-roll bar fitted to front suspension.

2 533 139 (Aug)
Solex 28 PCI carburettor modified and installed with distributor with vacuum advance only.

2 725 501 (Nov)
Valve stem strengthened at the point where it is welded to the valve head.

The start of a new decade saw a wild escalation in sales figures. Against a social, economic and political background that was so much more buoyant than any other period in human history, the Beetle became a huge success throughout every continent. While European, American and British manufacturers continued to launch completely new models in an attempt to increase sales, Volkswagen retained the Beetle's basic format except that, throughout the 1960s, Wolfsburg's engineering and design teams were kept busier than ever before. To the layman, of course, the Beetle for the 1961 model year was almost indistinguishable from the previous year's cars, but to the increasingly enthusiastic Beetle-buying public the latest offering from Wolfsburg was really a completely different model.

Naturally, the body remained virtually unchanged, but all cars destined for the British and European markets now abandoned semaphore indicators. The B-posts were smoothed out and the Beetle was, at long last, fitted with modern flashing indicators. Although very different from the units fitted to the American Export cars five years earlier, the new indicators were a great improvement from a safety point of view. Mounted on top of the front wings were narrow chrome-plated pods with amber lenses, the whole unit closely resembling a teardrop. At the rear, the indicators were housed in slightly larger stop and tail-light pods, but the lenses were yet to receive a separate amber segment to distinguish the indicators from the two other functions. At the same time, the plastic wing beading and the rubber covers on the running boards were colour-matched to the paintwork.

Inside the car, the ignition switch was fitted with a safety-inspired locking device similar to those found on all modern cars, which demanded that you turn the key back to 'base' in the event of the engine not firing first time. Incidentally, the ignition switch was not moved for the right-hand drive cars, which is why drivers with short arms found themselves having to stretch across the car to turn the key, an inconvenience which continued until the advent of the 12-volt cars in 1967. Another interior change was the inclusion of a soft plastic grab handle fitted to the passenger's side of the dashboard, although perhaps seat belts would have been preferable.

Although the flat-four engine retained a capacity of 1192cc, more power was extracted from it due to several detail changes and an increase in compression ratio from 6.6:1 to 7.0:1. The new engine, which had been introduced in the Type 2 Transporter in May 1959, has very few parts that are interchangeable with the earlier power unit, the modifications including a more rugged crankcase, a stronger crankshaft, a detachable dynamo pedestal, greater spacing of the cylinder barrels and a modified fuel pump drive. The cylinder heads were also redesigned with

CHASSIS DATING

Jan	2 862 052
Feb	2 922 174
Mar	2 988 365
Apr	3 048 367
May	3 115 196
Jun	3 178 360
Jul	3 204 566
Aug	3 267 185
Sep	3 335 847
Oct	3 405 533
Nov	3 478 068
Dec	3 551 044

TECHNICAL OUTLINE

1192cc 34bhp
Capacity 1192cc
Bore and stroke 77×64mm
Compression ratio 7:1
Carburettor Solex 28 PICT up to November 1963, 28 PICT/1 up to July 1970, 30 PICT up to 1978.
Max power 34bhp at 3600rpm
Gear ratios
1st 3.80:1
2nd 2.06:1
3rd 1.32:1
4th 0.89:1
Reverse 3.88:1
Final drive ratio 4.375:1

For the 1961 model year, both the saloon and cabriolet lost their semaphore indicators and gained modern flasher units on top of the front wings. This delightful cabriolet is owned by Danny Hermans.

wedge-shaped combustion chambers and the valves were placed at a slant.

Bore and stroke remained identical to the older engine, but power output went up from 30bhp to 34bhp. The new engine was also a little quieter thanks to a reduction in the speed of the cooling fan, achieved by using a larger dynamo pulley and a smaller crankshaft pulley. The 34bhp engine also demanded different tappet clearances, modified from .004in on the 30bhp engine to .008in for both inlet and exhaust.

For the 1961 model year, the Solex 28 PCI carburettor was replaced by the 28 PICT, which was fitted with a thermostatically-controlled automatic choke (said by some to have been responsible for increasing the car's fuel consumption) controlled by a bi-metallic spring and heated by a heater element. To improve cold starting further, the left-hand heat exchanger was modified so that a flexible card-type hose could be fitted to it, the purpose being to utilise warm air from the exchanger and direct it to the air cleaner on top of the carburettor. At the same time, the air cleaner was modified to include an intake fitted with a weighted flap valve in order to feed the carburettor with warm air during cold weather. This modification went some way towards preventing carburettor icing, but did not eradicate the problem altogether.

Again following the lead of the Type 2 Transporter in May 1959, the Beetle was fitted with a new gearbox. Apart from gaining synchromesh on all four forward gears, it had a redesigned one-piece casing (similar to the one employed on the Porsche 356) and revised ratios on third and fourth gears. The ratios are as follows: first, 3.80:1; second, 2.06:1; third, 1.32:1; fourth, 0.89:1; reverse, 3.88:1; final drive, 4.375:1.

One particularly welcome addition in March was a steering damper, which made a real improvement to the feel of the Beetle on the road. Exceptionally strong and well-made, a steering damper should last a very long time indeed, but a worn item will make its presence felt in no uncertain terms. Replacements are cheap and easy to fit, a Koni-made unit being even better than the original if you are lucky enough to find one.

The eight-fuse fusebox was removed from the luggage compartment behind the dashboard to the interior of the car beneath the dash, and was fitted with a plastic cover.

Mention should be made at this point of the Standard Beetle, which was not fitted with the uprated engine in 1960. By August 1960, indeed differences between the Standard and Export models became particularly pronounced as the former continued to be fitted with a crash gearbox and even retained cable brakes, hydraulics not arriving until April 1962, 12 years after the Export model was updated.

Intended to provide real economy motoring, the Standard was not fitted with a steering damper or front anti-roll bar, and the bumpers, door handles, hubcaps and tail pipes were painted rather than chromed. Body moulding strips were conspicuously absent and a three-spoke steering wheel was fitted instead of the two-spoke version.

The majority of Standard Beetles were sold in Germany. They were never officially exported to the USA, although there were some private imports and sales elsewhere were negligible. Today, these austere and basic cars are particularly coveted by 'vintage' enthusiasts, who claim that they are more representative of a true People's *wagen*. The 'people', however, voted with their pockets, for the Export or de luxe model outsold the Standard vehicle many times over. Interestingly, 30bhp Standard cars tend to be faster than 30bhp de luxe models for the simple reason that they are a good deal lighter.

Over the years, the Standard model was updated and modified, more or less along the same lines as the Export Beetle. After 30 October 1964, when it was fitted with the synchromesh gearbox, the two cars were very similar save that the Standard (or 1200A as it was known from then on), as its name suggests, was more basic in its level of trim.

In August 1966, production of the 34bhp 1200 model was temporarily halted although the 1200 engine was available in the 1300 to special order at that time. Production of the 1200 resumed in January 1967, and from then on it would be known as the 'Economy Beetle'.

PRODUCTION CHANGES
1960

2 921 552 (Feb)
Steering damper introduced.

3 060 711 (May)
Synthetic heater tubes with noise suppressors between body and engine.

3 116 871 (Jun)
Depressions in the spring plate hub to prevent horizontal movement of rear torsion bars.

3 192 507 (Jul)
Flashing indicators fitted to non-US cars; non-repeat ignition/starter switch; passenger grab handle on dashboard; oil pressure switch no longer adjustable; new eight-fuse fusebox with transparent cover now near steering column, previously behind dashboard; windscreen washer combined with wiper switch; headlamps changed from symmetric low beams to asymmetric low beams; 1192cc 30bhp engine replaced by 1192cc 34bhp unit, compression ratio increased from 6.6:1 to 7.0:1; dynamo pedestal now detachable rather than being cast into crankcase; synchromesh on all four forward gears, one-piece gearbox casing; 28 PICT carburettor with automatic choke replaces 28 PCI.

3 335 848 (Oct)
Boge shock absorbers become 35 per cent softer (rear).

3 341 077 (Oct)
Boge shock absorbers become 26 per cent softer (front).

3 405 001 (Oct)
Accelerator pedal mounted higher and rubber cover lengthened at base.

3 503 952 (Dec)
Fichtel & Sachs shock absorbers become 35 per cent softer (rear).

Introduced in August 1960, the revised 1192cc engine was uprated from 30bhp to 34bhp, the Solex 28 PICT carburettor had an automatic choke, and pre-heated air was fed through a tube from the heat exchanger to the air filter to improve engine performance at low revs.

COLOURS

From August 1960
Black
Ruby Red
Gulf Blue
Pearl White
Turquoise
Pastel Blue
Beryl Green

1961

CHASSIS DATING	
Jan	3 628 283
Feb	3 701 251
Mar	3 780 308
Apr	3 860 285
May	3 919 200
Jun	4 000 004
Jul	4 020 589
Aug	4 090 311
Sep	4 165 011
Oct	4 245 397
Nov	4 321 188
Dec	4 400 051

For the 1962 model year, the body remained the same but detail improvements continued as usual and included an amber segment in the rear lights for the indicator function.

The numerous developments this year were aimed at making the Beetle more 'user-friendly'. Looking back, it is arguably true to say that the Beetle began to lose even more of its original character but, looking on the bright side, the cars of the 1960s were better equipped and much more fun to drive.

The Beetle was little changed externally save that the rear lights gained an amber segment at the top of the lenses to distinguish the indicators from the stop and tail lights. Under the skin, the bonnet was supported for the first time by spring-loaded self-supporting struts on both sides – a practical and long overdue solution to a nail-biting irritation. One problem with the early cars was that well-intentioned non-VW folk, upon offering to close the bonnet for you, would do so without releasing the retaining clip on the stay, thereby making a fine job of bending your bonnet. Also under the bonnet, the washer bottle, introduced in August 1960, gained a valve which, when attached to an air-line, allowed the bottle to be pressurised.

Circular grommets were fitted to the heelboard panels to allow hot air into the rear of the car at ankle level. At the same time the vents in the front footwell were each fitted with a sliding steel cover with a small handle to the rear. The adjustable covers served two purposes: they not only allowed fine tuning of the amount of hot air entering the footwells, but also, by blanking off the outlets completely, enabled a greater quantity of warm air to be released through the vents below the windscreen.

Despite many claims to the contrary, the Volkswagen's heating and demisting system is extremely effective unless 'aftermarket' or non-genuine heat exchangers are fitted or the car is driven in such a way that the engine never reaches its proper operating temperature. In other words, the faster you drive, the hotter the car gets.

The Beetle was also fitted in 1961 with seat belt anchorage points, but you had to buy the seat belts separately. Although most of the cars built during this period encountered by this author are not fitted with seat belts, a prospective owner may like to consider a set out of a sense of self-preservation. But you would have to ask yourself whether you want to retain originality by purchasing the old-fashioned 'hang-loose' type or save yourself the possibility of chipping the paintwork on the outside of the rear quarter panels by fitting inertia reels. Having battled with seemingly endless yards of anarchic shoulder

The rubber covers on top of the running boards were colour matched to the bodywork for some paint colours, but black became universal across the range for the 1968 model year.

A spring-loaded strut on each side of the car replaced the single bonnet stay of previous Beetles.

COLOURS

From August 1961
Black
Anthracite
Ruby Red
Gulf Blue
Turquoise
Pearl White
Beryl Green
Pacific

These colours were
current for two model
years

To the left of the 90mph speedometer (or to the right on left-hand drive cars), a fuel gauge replaced the reserve tap in the passenger footwell, and a push button was integrated into the windscreen wiper knob to operate the pressurised windscreen washer bottle. The passenger grab handle had been added to the dashboard in 1960.

The familiar vents in the front footwells were fitted with sliding steel covers to regulate the flow of air.

The seat rails were lengthened and a greater range of adjustment was possible for the front seats with the cranked knob at the base of the seat frame.

straps for years, modern inertia reels get my vote every time.

By far the most useful modification for this year's new car was the addition of a fuel gauge, which resulted in the reserve tap in the footwell being dropped – and not before time. Fitted to the right of the speedometer on left-hand drive cars and to the left on right-hookers, the instrument was square, in contrast to the round speedometer, and trimmed around its perimeter with a polished aluminium moulding in keeping with the dashboard trim.

The worm and peg steering box employed since the pre-war prototypes was replaced by a worm and roller system, a great improvement which offered easier operation and better directional control. This unit operates with an hour-glass worm in combination with a roller mounted on needle bearings. Unlike the worm and peg system, it is practically drag-free as the contact between the worm and roller is no longer in the nature of sliding friction.

PRODUCTION CHANGES 1961

3 616 527 (Jan)
Thrust surface for distributor drive shaft 5mm deeper in left-hand half of crankcase.

3 627 442 (Jan)
Fan pulley ratios altered from 1.8:1 to 1.75:1.

3 806 249 (Apr)
Connection hose from oil filler to oil bath cleaner for crankcase ventilation, instead of breather tube.

3 856 472 (Apr)
Stop/tail lights and indicators in twin-segment lens on de luxe and Standard Beetle in Germany only.

3 933 185 (Jun)
Worm and roller steering introduced.

4 010 995 (Jul)
Spring-loaded struts to support bonnet; warm air outlets added to heelboards and vents in front footwells given sliding shutters; seat belt anchorage points fitted; fuel gauge introduced on Export saloon and cabriolet in place of reserve tap; twin-segment rear lights for all export markets; green indicator light for flashing indicator warning lamp (previously red).

4 040 690 (Aug)
Clutch operating lever with splines fixed to shaft with circlip instead of clamp screw.

4 089 142 (Aug)
Left and right tie rods adjustable and maintenance-free on Export model.

4 166 056 (Oct)
Automatic cooling air regulation, operating temperature of thermostat 65-70°C (previously 75-80°).

4 289 952 (Nov)
Gear knob conical and smaller.

1962

Whereas cars made before December 1962 relied on air being passed over the engine for heating the cabin, those made after this date were fitted with heat exchangers and can be distinguished by the two thick pipes on the right and left.

This was a vintage year in some respects, although enthusiasts mourned the passing of the famous Wolfsburg crest bonnet badge, a move that symbolised the severing of yet another link with the car's history. Apart from that, the badge added just a little something to the Beetle's identity which the V-over-W emblem failed to equal. The Count of Schulenburg's castle, however, continued on the steering wheel hub, so not all was lost.

As a result of the crest's removal, the central moulding on the bonnet was extended down towards the handle and a more prominent and improved version of the V-over-W motif was fitted at the top of the bonnet near the front bulkhead. In recent times, the Beetle has both enjoyed and suffered from a massive revival in popularity, as we all know, and VW bonnet badges in particular have become targets for thieves of questionable parentage and stunted evolutionary development.

During the later 1980s, thousands of badges were stolen from Beetles and other Volkswagen models by younger people attempting to identify themselves more closely with a pop group, the Beastie Boys, who were enjoying some success at the time with their version of modern music. The connection between the group and Volkswagen badges is something of an enigma and, although the craze seems to be over, the V-over-W emblem is still far from safe from the late developers who have not quite grasped the ephemeral nature of what passes for fashion.

Apart from badging, the bodywork was indistinguishable from the previous year's car, but there were internal differences. The most significant modification was a new vinyl headlining. Coloured white with tiny black spots, it was not only easier to keep clean than the cloth materials used previously, but it also gave the cabin an altogether more spacious and airy feel. While it reduced the 'cosy' factor still further, the new-look interior reflected perfectly the age in which it belonged. The circular heater vents in the rear heel board panels were each fitted with a moveable flap operated by a small stalk-like handle which enabled rear passengers to regulate the flow of heat around their ankles.

On the mechanical front, there was a breath of fresh air for the heating system. Until the middle of December 1962, heat for the cabin was provided by hot air passing over the cylinders and cylinder heads and by heater 'elements' or boxes that formed part of the exhaust pipes exiting from the front pair of cylinders (numbers one and three). When heat was required inside the car, you simply unscrewed the cable-operated control knob on the backbone tunnel, thereby shutting the cooling air outlet flap and opening the heat control valve. The warm air was then directed through to the six outlets in the cabin.

This system was redesigned for 1963 and heat exchangers were fitted so that fresh air could be provided, thus avoiding the possibility of blowing exhaust and oil fumes into the car. The two heat exchangers are mounted below the cylinders, one heat exchanger below each pair of cylinders. Made from sheet steel, they are simple chambers through the middle of which passes the exhaust pipe from

The enamel bonnet badge depicting Wolfsburg Castle was dropped in 1962 and the alloy moulding was brought closer to the top of the bonnet handle.

1963

each of the front cylinders. Blown through a hose on the fan housing by the fan, air surrounding the exhaust pipes within the chambers is ducted through pipes to the cabin.

If fumes do enter the cabin, remedial action should be taken immediately. Checks should be made for engine oil leaks and for leaks at the flanges between the exhaust pipes, tailbox and tail pipes. Dirty cylinder barrels, cylinder head cooling fins or a dirty oil cooler can obviously lead to a rise in engine temperatures, engine damage and the likelihood of fumes being blown into the car. Although genuine Volkswagen heat exchangers last for many years, tailboxes usually need replacing every three years or so. When rust sets in and makes holes in the exhaust system, you may smell fumes inside the car as well as being subjected to the most excruciatingly awful racket from the engine.

PRODUCTION CHANGES 1962

4 388 450 (Jan)
Rear wheel bearings – inner spacer ring thickness 6.45-6.65mm (previously 5.9-6.1mm).

4 545 651 (Mar)
Breather pipe connected to reservoir of oil bath cleaner, previously on air intake.

4 570 540 (Mar)
Outer surface of manifold and pre-heater pipe treated with zinc paint, previously phosphated.

4 630 938 (Apr)
Hydraulic brakes replace mechanical brakes on Standard model.

4 636 869 (Apr)
Fuel pipe between pump and carburettor with flexible connecting pieces, rubber tubing with textile outer covering previously.

4 671 926 (Apr)
Door hinges fitted to bodywork with three screws, previously four.

4 750 946 (May)
Valve springs become 'progressively coiled'.

4 846 836 (Jul)
Vinyl replaces woolcloth for headlining.

4 874 267 (Aug)
Oil fumes conducted into oil bath air cleaner, previously into open air.

4 981 020 (Sep)
Vacuum pipe increased from 310mm to 375mm.

5 010 448 (Oct)
Wolfsburg crest on bonnet lid discontinued.

5 112 045 (Nov)
Rubber bush for spring plate hub modified in size and increased in volume.

5 188 470 (Dec)
Rear compartment heater vents fitted with regulating flaps.

5 199 980 (Dec)
Air for cabin heating heated in heat exchangers, previously heated by cylinders.

Even the 'teardrop' shape of the front indicators, introduced for the 1961 model year and later to be widened in October 1963, was in keeping with the car's overall curvaceous styling.

Opening rear side windows were a rare option on cars exported to Britain and other countries with a cold climate.

Having spent the past couple of years working overtime perfecting their People's car and keeping themselves busy with the launch of the Type 3 saloon in 1961, Wolfsburg's engineers appear to have awarded themselves something of a rest for 1963 – and who could blame them? The 1963 cars certainly carried modifications, but they were largely confined to cosmetics and you have to be an enthusiast to spot them.

The pretty Pope's nose, a minor component which in itself had been subjected to a number of detail modifications over the years, was dropped and replaced by a very much wider and flatter pod housing above the registration plate. The engine lid was slightly modified to accept the new pod. The indicator pods up front were also widened so they could be seen more easily by other motorists, but they retained a streamlined teardrop shape.

The beautifully made domed hubcaps, which were just two years away from being discontinued in favour of less shapely items, no longer came with their centrally positioned V-over-W emblems painted in black. This was a cost-cutting exercise which doubtless saved Volkswagen many gallons of paint and obviously resulted in many owners doing the job themselves, or having their dealers do it for them. So, if you come across a post-August 1963 Beetle with hubcaps that have black VW emblems, please do not be surprised or in a hurry to condemn it on the grounds of lack of originality. Not all modifications carried out at Wolfsburg were in the nature of improvements.

From August, the Export model was offered with an optional sliding steel sunroof in place of the roll-top variety, but the latter, being cheaper, continued as an option on the basic Standard model. Opened manually with a handle, the new sunroof is very much smaller than the vinyl sunroofs and has a tendency to rust to the point of being inoperable. Restoring a steel sunroof, therefore, can be a tricky operation which has led more than one or two sober devotees in the direction of the drinks cabinet before now. Indeed, one enthusiast known to this author became so exasperated with his attempts to repair the sunroof on his car that he eventually cut out the whole unit and welded in a new roof panel.

Inside the car, the seat covers were changed from cloth to harder-wearing vinyl, and the semi-circular horn rim was temporarily discarded so that the horn was operated by pressing elongated chrome-plated buttons set into the two spokes.

It is interesting that Beetle production was down from more than 867,000 cars in 1962 to less than 839,000 in 1963, but would rise for the first time to well over a million in 1965 after the introduction of the 1300 model. It seems that the 1200 was beginning to decrease in popularity as society became more affluent.

Jo Clay's nicely restored Beetle, built in September 1963, is bodily the same as the cars of the previous year except that the hubcap emblems are no longer picked out in black, but one important change under the skin from December 1962 was a new 'fresh air' heating system.

For many enthusiasts, Bob Wynn's red 1200 cabriolet, manufactured in April 1964, is the ultimate expression of the Beetle theme. Elegant understated styling combined with the traditional torsion bar chassis must surely rate this Beetle as one of the most desirable.

The semi-circular horn rim was discontinued in 1963, only to reappear again on the 1300 in 1965.

The reinforcing panel at the bottom of the engine lid (below), which was discontinued on the 1966 1500, is a common source of corrosion if the water drainage holes become blocked. For the 1964 model year, the registration light pod (below left) became much broader and flatter. The cabriolet engine lid differs, as always, in containing intake louvres which after 1957 were slatted horizontally rather than vertically. Note that this British-registered car is fitted with American-spec bumpers.

PRODUCTION CHANGES 1963

5 239 191 (Jan)
Hemscheidt steering damper gains inner sealing lip with spiral ring.

5 261 830 (Jan)
Clutch cable shortened by 10mm.

5 578 122 (Jun)
Petrol injected into cylinders by 28 PICT carburettor increased from 1.1cc to 1.4cc per accelerator pump stroke.

5 661 082 (Jul)
Heat-resistant clutch pressure springs introduced.

5 677 119 (Aug)
Rear registration light pod made wider; semi-circular horn rim replaced by twin chrome-plated buttons; optional sunroof now sliding steel for Export model; seat covers changed from cloth to vinyl; hubcaps no longer highlighted in black.

5 813 842 (Sep)
Rear shock absorbers from Hoesch with PVC synthetic protective tubes.

5 888 185 (Oct)
Front indicators widened.

5 909 656 (Nov)
Oil bath air cleaner modified with depression on lower part of filter to make way for enlarged automatic choke mechanism.

COLOURS

From August 1963
Black
Ruby Red
Sea Blue
Pearl White
Anthracite

Apart from the metalwork above the door panels, the cabriolet's interior is virtually indistinguishable from the saloon's.

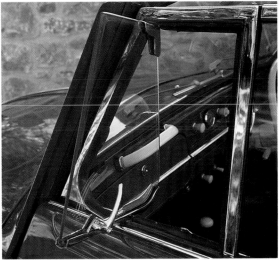

Beautifully maintained upholstery which is typical of the cars from this period (right). Note that the cabriolet differs from the saloon in having winders in the side panels to operate the rear windows. To allow for the shape of the hood, the frames around the cabriolet's quarterlights (far right) are more angular than those of the saloon.

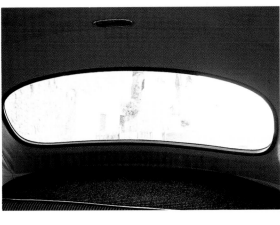

The cabriolet's rear window (right), always made of glass, was progressively enlarged over the years to keep pace with the saloon. With its external vinyl material and plastic headlining sandwiching a horsehair and rubber filling, the high quality, simple-to-operate hood (far right) remained the same as ever.

1964

This was another year of significant change, yet the modifications were so subtle that a casual observer could be forgiven for thinking that the latest Beetle was just the same as ever. Take a close look above the waistline, however, and the major alterations to the bodywork are readily apparent. With the aim of increasing all-round visibility, all the windows were increased in size, and for the first time the windscreen was curved – but only slightly – instead of being flat.

By reducing the width of the A-posts, forward visibility and thus safety was certainly improved, but again a small amount of character was lost and that is reflected in today's prices for these cars. In an attempt by Volkswagen to remain competitive, the Beetle was becoming less like the sleek insect from which it took its nickname. Yet production continued to rise to meet worldwide demand and reached over one million units in 1965.

As a result of enlarging the windscreen, the wiper blades were lengthened accordingly and instead of 'parking' on the right as previously, they were modified to come to rest on the left-hand side of the windscreen. This change was a benefit to right-hand drive cars, but despite the new arrangement a segment of the windscreen remained out of reach of the right-hand wiper and continued to make life a little difficult on right-hand corners in adverse weather conditions. The frames between the quarterlights and the door windows were sloped at an angle rather than being vertical as on the previous models, and the T-shaped engine lid handle, which some people surprisingly found awkward to use, was replaced by a lockable push-button unit.

To increase the volume of usable luggage space inside the car, the backrest of the rear seat could now be folded forward to the horizontal position. This was a great idea, but with the backrest folded engine noise levels in the cabin increased. The cars made up to August were also the last to be fitted with a single heater knob. For the new model year, the Beetle was fitted with two handles mounted side by side to the rear of the handbrake; they lay flat when the heater

was not in use. When pulled upwards, the handle on the right (with a red knob on its end) allowed heat into the car through all six outlets, whereas the handle on the left (fitted with a white knob) controlled the two outlets in the rear, in effect superseding the manually operated levers in the rear footwells of the previous year's cars.

PRODUCTION CHANGES 1964

115 000 001 (Aug)
All windows enlarged; folding rear seat backrest introduced; heater operation now by two levers; push button latch for engine lid; sun visors larger and with different mountings; needle bearings for gears arranged in pairs (previously single).

115 004 037 (Aug)
Automatic cooling air regulation: four flaps inside fan housing on pressure side, previously throttle ring in front of fan.

115 084 567 (Sep)
Warm air hose increased from 55mm to 60mm in diameter; heat exchangers fitted with internally ribbed exhaust pipes.

115 162 787 (Oct)
Clutch plate: splines in hub now given phosphated sliding finish.

115 217 625 (Oct)
Steering worm with marking ring for adjustment.

115 247 529 (Oct)
Synchromesh on all four forward gears for 1200A or Standard model.

115 255 751 (Nov)
Rocker arm: outer oil drilling on valve adjustment screw welded (previously open).

115 331 161 (Dec)
Spark plugs now Champion L87y, Bosch W175T 1 or Beru 175/14.

115 336 420 (Dec)
Oil bath air cleaner with crankcase breather pipe for 1200A model (previously none).

115 349 565 (Dec)
Windscreen wiper arms fitted with tension spring in place of compression spring.

CHASSIS DATING

Jan	6 092 060
Feb	6 182 046
Mar	6 240 170
Apr	6 321 709
May	6 391 125
Jun	6 479 490
Jul	6 502 399
Aug	115 073 129
Sep	115 161 387
Oct	115 252 151
Nov	115 331 160
Dec	115 410 000

COLOURS

From August 1964
Fontana Grey
Ruby Red
Sea Blue
Pearl Grey
Black
Panama Beige
Java Green
Bahama Blue

Although changes above the waistline are subtle, all the windows were enlarged, the windscreen became curved instead of flat (far left), and the A-posts were slimmer. The longer wipers now parked on the right, a benefit to visibility on right-hand drive cars. The familiar single heater knob (left) disappeared in August 1964, to be replaced by two parallel handles behind the handbrake.

1965

CHASSIS DATING

Jan	115 500 000
Feb	115 574 322
Mar	115 678 203
Apr	115 767 035
May	115 861 066
Jun	115 967 150
Jul	115 979 202
Aug	116 102 780
Sep	116 204 348
Oct	116 302 145
Nov	116 382 728
Dec	116 463 103

TECHNICAL OUTLINE

1300 (single-port)
Capacity 1285cc
Bore and stroke 77×69mm
Compression ratio 7.3:1
Carburettor Solex 30 PICT
Max power 40bhp at 4000rpm
Gear ratios
1st 3.80:1
2nd 2.06:1
3rd 1.32:1
4th 0.89:1,
Reverse 3.88:1
Final drive ratio 4.375:1

By the mid-1960s, Volkswagen had come a very long way indeed since the dark and primitive days of the immediate post-war period. Hard work had paid large dividends in terms of sales both at home and abroad, but suddenly the world was a very different place. The threat of increased competition in the small-to-medium car market, particularly from the Japanese, loomed large on the horizon, and the days in which Volkswagen could rely solely on the 1200 Beetle for its continued existence and success were coming to an end.

With just 34bhp on tap, the Beetle was grossly underpowered. Although production of the 1200 continued, the new 1300 model added to the range offered an extra 6bhp, which admittedly did not project the Beetle into 'supercar' territory but the increase in power was nevertheless an extremely worthwhile improvement.

The increased engine capacity was achieved by utilising the crankshaft from the Type 3 1500 Volkswagen to lengthen the stroke from 64mm to 69mm, giving an overall capacity of 1285cc. To ensure that the engine remained under-stressed, the cylinder heads continued to breathe through single-port inlets despite the fact that tuning companies like Okrasa had been producing an excellent twin-port conversion for many years. The compression ratio was also up from 7:1 to 7.3:1, and the maximum 40bhp was produced at 4000rpm.

Despite a 17½ per cent increase in power over the 1200, 0-60mph acceleration in around 23sec meant that the Beetle was still losing ground to competitors like the Ford Cortina and Renault 1100. However, Volkswagen was quick to point out in its handbooks that the great advantage of the Beetle was that its maximum speed was also its cruising speed, which meant you could drive the car at 76mph all day every day for many years.

While contemporary road tests in English and American journals complimented the new car on its build quality, improved performance and slick gearchange, several motoring writers continued to criticise the 'awkward' positioning of the pedals, which remained hinged at the bottom rather than at the top as on conventional cars. Dyed-in-the-wool Beetle folk know only too well that the pedal cluster is just about perfect and that conventional arrangements are 'all wrong'.

Externally, the car was little changed except for a new 1300 badge on the left-hand side of the engine lid, but the revised car was nevertheless considerably more than a 1200 Beetle with a 1300 engine. The many detail modifications were designed to increase the car's appeal across the board.

To improve windscreen demisting, an additional vent was incorporated into the top of the dashboard, the 'hole' containing a black plastic insert for the sake of neatness. The semi-circular horn rim, last seen in July 1963, made a comeback. The floor-operated headlight dipswitch was at last built into a

The semi-circular horn rim made a comeback with the introduction of the 1300 and an additional vent was fitted in the middle of the dashboard to improve windscreen demisting.

Despite having covered a high mileage, this car's interior and, more particularly, its seats are still in pristine condition. Note that the chrome strip on the door panel is now slightly lower down than on 1950s Beetles.

stalk on the left-hand side of the steering column for the 1300. Safety features included a lock incorporated in the front seat backrest adjusters (to prevent them tilting forward in the event of an accident), anti-burst door locks and stronger seat mountings.

Not for the first time in its life, the front suspension was refined. Although the beam layout remained, the king-pin and link-pin assemblies were dropped in favour of ball joints, and ten torsion leaves were employed instead of eight. Despite the increase in engine power, the existing 9in diameter drum brakes of the 1200 were found to offer adequate stopping power, but the drums were strengthened with star-shaped ribs for protection against potential heat distortion.

Ventilated road wheels were introduced on the 1300 saloon and cabriolet. Apart from improving the

appearance of the car and allowing slightly better cooling for the brakes, these also reduced unsprung weight. And to finish the wheels, there was a new set of chromed hubcaps which were flatter than the domed ones fitted to the 1200s previously.

Strangely, the wheels and brake drums of the 1300s produced during 1965 and 1966 are partially responsible for the rarity of these cars today. A number of years ago, a British-based company, GP Specialist Vehicles of Isleworth, launched a low-volume glass-fibre copy of Porsche's 1959 Porsche 718 RSK, based on a Beetle floorpan. It was quickly discovered that the 1300 Beetle formed an ideal basis for the kit car as its brake drums and wheels, when painted metallic silver, closely resembled those of the RSK Porsche. Some Beetles were broken up to form 'donor' cars.

A 1300 badge set at an angle on the engine lid distinguishes the more powerful car from its 34bhp 1200 sister.

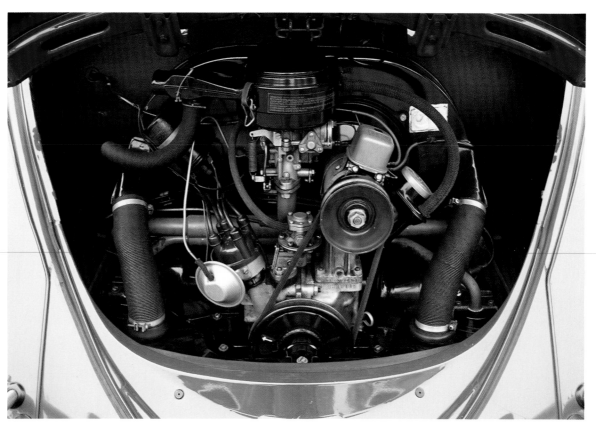

A genuine 1300 single-port engine has an 'F' prefix to the engine serial number, which is clearly visible stamped on the crankcase below the generator pedestal. Lengthening the stroke from 64mm to 69mm took engine capacity to 1285cc for the new 1300 model, and helped to raise power by 6bhp to 40bhp. Having had one fastidious owner from new, this car retains a remarkably original engine compartment.

PRODUCTION CHANGES 1965

COLOURS

From August 1965
Sea Blue
VW Blue
Fontana Grey
Black
Ruby Red
Sea Blue
Pearl White
Java Green
Bahama Blue
Sea Sand

115 594 027 (Mar)
Ignition cables now with copper cores, resistor for spark plug connector (1 kilo-ohm) and suppressed distributor (previously resistor type ignition cable).

115 685 587 (Apr)
Clutch operating arm now straight with wing nut to adjust clutch cable (previously curved with hexagonal nut for adjustment).

115 720 690 (Apr)
Valve spring caps now with thick walls and sharply defined guide shoulder; previously thin walls with flatter guide shoulder.

115 928 504 (Jun)
Standard 1200 fitted with spring-loaded bonnet struts, previously single arm with manual lock.

116 000 001 (Aug)
Horn rim reintroduced on new 1300 Beetle; headlight dip-switch placed on steering column; additional dashboard vent for windscreen demisting; safety lock for front seat backrests; anti-burst door locks; 1200 and 1300 engines given bearing shells for camshaft; shaft of heater control flap galvanised; oil return thread cast into gearbox casing in front of main drive shaft oil seal; spacing between front torsion bar tubes increased from 120mm to 150mm; number of torsion leaves at front increased from eight to ten; steering knuckle connected to torsion arms with maintenance-free ball joints; upper ball joints in eccentric bush with which camber can be set; front wheel bearings now tapered roller bearings (previously angular thrust ball bearings).

116 240 000 (Oct)
Solex 30 PICT-1 fitted to 1300 with longer accelerator pump connecting rod provided with two holes for the cotter pin and spring.

To prevent the door flying open in the event of a heavy collision, a safety lock (right) was fitted above the main door lock mechanism. This style of exterior handle, with a round push button, was not introduced until 1966. Another safety feature introduced on the 1300 was a special lock (far right) fitted at the base of the seat to prevent the backrest folding forward.

1966

If the 1300 Beetle introduced in 1965 marked a mild departure from conventional Volkswagen wisdom, the 1500 launched for the 1967 model year was positively wild. Dubbed the 'Hot Beetle' in some quarters, the six-volt 1500s are today among the most sought-after of all air-cooled Volkswagens not only because of their aesthetic appeal but also because they more or less combine the legendary reliability of the 1200 with the performance of the later 1600 versions.

Almost everything about the 'Fifteen', as it is affectionately known, was very different from the cars that preceded it, and in many ways from those that succeeded it too. It was a real driver's car: although its performance, on paper, was not quite on a par with many of its contemporaries, a skilled driver prepared to wring every ounce of power from the engine could really make it fly. Handling and road-holding were also improved to the point where, even in standard form, the 1500 could be made to 'talk' to the road, provided the standard crossply tyres were scrapped in favour of a decent set of radials, such as Michelins.

To meet the requirements of new American legislation, the engine lid was modified so that it sat slightly higher on the valance and allowed the registration plate to be positioned more vertically. In effect, the engine lid was bent in the middle, but surely not for the purpose of creating more room for the larger engine as was suggested in the press at the time of the car's launch in August. The curvaceous engine lid also had a VW 1500 badge positioned on the left-hand side.

The bright trim adorning the bodywork at waist level, on the outside of the running boards and on the bonnet was made very much narrower and the door handles gained round press buttons which could be locked with the ignition key. Until this time, a separate key was required, inconveniently, for the door locks.

Inside the car, the sides of the backrests of the front seats were fitted with levers to make it easier to tilt them forward – no more bending down to operate the locking mechanism. The steering wheel and control knobs were coloured black to help prevent distracting reflections in the windscreen. The con-

Arguably the very best Beetle ever made, the 1500, introduced in August 1966, is a real driver's car. It is fast, handles exceptionally well and is equipped with powerful front disc brakes. Stuart Andrews owns this sparkling example.

COLOURS

From August 1966
Fontana Grey
Ruby Red
Pearl White
VW Blue
Savanna Beige
Zenith Blue
Black
Java Green
Lotus White

By this stage in the car's production, the seats were upholstered in a 'dimply' vinyl material, usually in black or white. The rear seats are vulnerable to splitting along their top edge.

CHASSIS DATING

Jan	116 543 112
Feb	116 622 320
Mar	116 723 045
Apr	116 809 563
May	116 909 207
Jun	116 1017 006
Jul	116 1021 298
Aug	117 109 832
Sep	117 202 292
Oct	117 288 898
Nov	117 363 979
Dec	117 422 503

trol knobs were all flatter and made of soft plastic in the hope that upon contact with a high-speed human, less damage would occur to the latter. The ashtray lost its pull-knob for the same reason.

For the first time, slim, elegant push-buttons were employed for locking the doors internally, while smaller interior door handles were fashioned as pull-out levers, instead of being pushed forwards and backwards as previously. The voltage regulator, which previously sat on top of the dynamo in the engine compartment, was repositioned under the left-hand side of the rear seat.

Genuine 1500 engines are distinguished by an 'H' prefix in front of the engine number, stamped on the crankcase below the dynamo pedestal – a point worth checking carefully if you are considering buying one of these fine cars. Notably more powerful than the 1300, the 1493cc single-port unit produces 44bhp at 4000rpm and the maximum torque of 78lb ft occurs at 2600rpm, offering more usable power across the range. Although the engine retained the 1300's 69mm stroke, the bore was enlarged from 77mm to 83mm. The compression ratio was also

increased to 7.5:1. Another feature of the six-volt 1500s is the 'twin-pronged' air cleaner, a modification made necessary because the intake pre-heating air was taken from *both* cylinder heads and directed to its destination via two flexible hoses.

From August 1966, the third gear ratio of all Beetles was revised to 1.26:1 to suit traffic conditions. The 1500 Beetles were fitted with a 4.125:1 rear axle ratio whereas the ratio of the 1300 was 4.375:1.

Apart from having a wider rear track, up from 1250mm on the 1200s of yesteryear to 1350mm on the 1500 and 1349mm on the 1300 and updated 1200, all three models were fitted at the rear with an equaliser spring (commonly but incorrectly referred to as an anti-roll bar) whose role is to provide additional help to the torsion bars under load. The spring, which runs transversely across the car under the rear luggage bay, is connected to each axle tube by rods and levers, and secured to the inner wing panels by rubber-bushed brackets. Although the spring did not reduce body roll, which was never a prominent Beetle problem anyway, it did improve the roadholding to such an extent that the car's

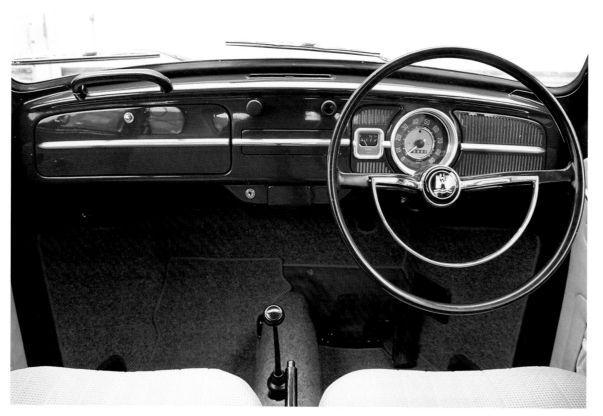

The last of the classic Beetle dashboards, which in the near future would be without a separate fuel gauge and the decorative alloy moulding. For 1966, flat control switches were in black plastic for greater safety and to prevent reflections in the windscreen.

Narrower door and body mouldings were introduced on the 1500, along with new door handles with round push buttons (far left). The doors were lockable from the inside with elegant plastic buttons on top of the window sill. A genuine 1500 has an 'H' prefix in front of the engine's serial number (left).

TECHNICAL OUTLINE

1500 (single port)
Capacity 1493cc
Bore and stroke 83×69mm
Compression ratio 7.5:1
Carburettor Solex 30 PICT 1
Max power 44bhp at 4000rpm
Gear ratios

1st	3.80:1
2nd	2.06:1
3rd	1.26:1
4th	0.89:1
Reverse	3.88:1

Final drive ratio 4.125:1

inherent tendency to oversteer, a regular criticism, was virtually eliminated overnight.

Another radical chassis change included the arrival of front disc brakes, but for the 1500 only. To Volkswagen's design, these brakes have 277mm diameter discs and calipers with pistons of 40mm diameter. The 1300 continued with all-round drums, and strangely soldiered on with the attractive but long-in-the-tooth five-stud road wheels, whereas the more powerful car came with four-stud items. Incidentally, all Beetles at this stage were still supplied to

dealers with crossply tyres which did little for customers wishing to take advantage of the new chassis modifications. Wisely, many enthusiasts changed to radials after wearing out the original rubber, which, in this author's experience, never took very long.

If you have a six-volt 1500, especially one in good condition, you can consider yourself very fortunate because many examples appear, sadly, to have rotted rather more quickly than earlier Beetles. Is it just a coincidence that the German economy went into recession in the mid-1960s?

A 'twin-pronged' air filter distinguishes the 44bhp engine of the 1500 from lesser models.

Apart from having a widened rear track, the Beetle was fitted for the 1967 model year with an ingenious equaliser spring (right), a device which provides assistance to the torsion bars under load. Initially, the 1500 was the only model to be equipped with front disc brakes (far right). To take advantage of them and the other chassis modifications, it is advisable to fit radial tyres.

PRODUCTION CHANGES
1966

116 851 572 (May)
Clutch and brake pedals fabricated from steel, previously cast iron.

116 866 804 (May)
Steering balljoint: material for plastic retaining ring for balljoint seal modified, internal diameter 3mm larger.

117 000 001 (Aug)
1500 Beetle introduced with significant engine, bodywork and interior modifications, as described in text;

power of new single-port 1493cc unit rises to 44bhp; fusebox increased from eight to ten fuses; windscreen wiper motor with two speeds and new rotary switch; flywheel increased from 109 to 130 teeth; starter motor and gearbox casing modified; 1500 Beetle fitted with front disc brakes; rear suspension fitted with equaliser spring and rear track increased on all models.

117 054 916 (Aug)
Oil pressure relief valve now piston with annular groove, previously without groove.

117 349 409 (Nov)
Brake fluid reservoir on 1500 positioned higher.

1967

With the departure of sloping headlights, 1967 marks an unofficial 'cut-off' date for enthusiasts and historians alike because the Beetle was radically altered in appearance in order to comply with increasingly stringent American safety legislation. Whereas the styling had previously looked elegant, curvaceous and happy, the latest arrival was beefy and its frontal appearance, although still happy and smiling, looked, thanks to the bigger bumpers, as though the car was biting on a hard piece of wood in an attempt to hide the pain. Despite being a better car, the new Beetle looked less confident about the future, even though production figures would continue to rocket and reach an all-time high of over 1.2 million in 1971.

Frankly, the Beetles produced up to 1970 were really quite brilliant and a good 1500 today is almost worth its weight in gold, but by this time other cars had not only caught up with the Beetle but had long since overtaken it. The far-sighted Volkswagen board began to search for a magic formula for a new and more modern replacement for the ageing Beetle, since the Type 3 saloon, launched in 1961, had not become as popular as expected.

That aside, the new Beetle for the 1968 model year received a major facelift and a whole host of detail modifications which, it was hoped, would put the car in a better position to compete with the new breed of economy cars from Japan. Beetle sales were undoubtedly aided by Walt Disney's film *The Love Bug* in which Herbie, the irrepressible Beetle, had a character and mind of its own. To my eternal regret, I was not able to see the film when it was originally

CHASSIS DATING	
Jan	117 505 826
Feb	117 566 719
Mar	117 620 975
Apr	117 674 558
May	117 739 188
Jun	117 817 896
Jul	117 844 902
Aug	118 077 888
Sep	118 160 490
Oct	118 258 722
Nov	118 351 958
Dec	118 431 603

A heavily revised 12-volt Beetle was introduced in both 1300 and 1500 forms in August 1967. Changes included vertical headlights set in modified wings, stronger and higher bumpers, bigger tail light units, a shorter engine lid and a host of other details aimed at improving safety and broadening the car's appeal. This 1500, owned by John Alexander, is an early semi-automatic, a transmission novelty which proved less popular than Volkswagen had hoped.

Fresh air ventilation was fed through louvres cut into the top of the bonnet (far left). This style of VW motif had been introduced in 1962, at the same time as the traditional Wolfsburg crest was dropped. From August 1967, the rubber covers on the running boards (left) were always black, rather than sometimes being coloured to match the paintwork.

released because of the huge number of Beetle-owning adults who filled the seats for a whole week. In fact, the cinema car park could easily have been mistaken for a small part of Wolfsburg throughout the duration of each showing and it was the same story everywhere else. 'Beetlemania' had indeed taken off in a big way.

The introduction of vertically positioned headlights meant that the front wings had to be modified accordingly, and the horn grilles were discontinued on both the 1300 and 1500. At the rear, the light pods and lenses were enlarged considerably, and built-in reversing lights – items rarely seen on cars in Britain – were offered as optional extras.

The larger bumpers were stronger and placed higher than the old blade type, a move which necessitated shortening both the bonnet and engine lid. In turn, the front and rear valances were lengthened and the front valance no longer had slots for the bumper brackets, which were subsequently mounted on the outside of the inner wings instead of the inside as previously.

Replacement bumpers are readily available, but it is worth taking the trouble to ensure that the items you buy are genuine Volkswagen-made bumpers. In recent times the market has been flooded with bumpers of such doubtful quality that Beetle folk have been moved to comment that their shiny new purchases do not last as long as the polythene in which they are wrapped. Genuine Volkswagen bumpers do not corrode in less than six months and are not plated in chrome that peels off in large chunks, but identifying the non-genuine items until this happens is not easy because they too are stamped with a 'look-alike' VW emblem. Naturally, Volkswagen dealerships only sell the real thing.

Also for the 1968 model year, the rubber covers on the running boards were no longer colour-matched to the body but were black across the range. The top of the bonnet was punctured with vents for the

A push button was incorporated at the bottom of the bonnet handle for the 1968 model year only.

A plastic box in front of the dashboard directed fresh air into the cabin and a flexible pipe running from the filler neck to the top of the fuel tank was installed.

For safety reasons, the door handles (right) were redesigned with a trigger release behind the handle. The fuel filler neck was relocated in the front inner wing (far right), so it was no longer necessary to open the bonnet at petrol stations. Initially the flap was not lockable and a finger cut-out was added in front of the flap.

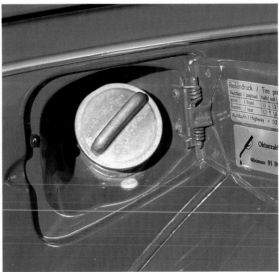

newly-introduced fresh-air system, the vents directing air into a plastic box behind the dashboard which in turn directs the flow through two flexible pipes to outlets on top of the dashboard. The decorative aluminium grilles offered as optional extras to cover these vents (and similar appendages for the rear louvres) look smart but are probably best avoided as they tend to trap water and encourage rust.

With the repositioning of the petrol filler neck in the right-hand front inner wing, it was no longer necessary to open the bonnet to fill up with five-star (or two-star if you preferred), but the filler flap was not lockable at this stage. The door handles were modified yet again: in place of the push buttons of the earlier 1500s, the latest cars had safety-inspired trigger releases placed out of harm's way behind the handles. Paradoxically, a push button was employed on the bonnet handle for this one model year only, although what advantage it offered is not easy to appreciate.

Inside the car, the ignition switch was moved from the dashboard and integrated into the steering column on the right-hand side, while the headlight flasher was now operated simply by pulling the column-mounted stalk – previously a separate button on the rear of the stalk operated the flasher. The petrol gauge, previously separate and positioned next to the speedometer, was now built in to the speedometer itself, a great pity because the result was a dashboard more barren in appearance than even the cars of 1945. A black padded dashboard, however, was offered as an option. In addition, two extra fresh air vents on top of the dashboard were each controlled by a rotating knob below the radio, and the gear lever returned to being straight (as with pre-1956 cars) instead of cranked.

The introduction of 12-volt electrics was long overdue. The entire system was uprated, including light bulbs, coil, dynamo and starter motor. To remind owners that their new steeds had been mod-

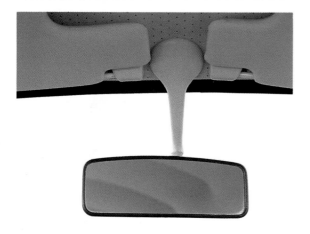

The plastic brake fluid reservoir (far left, top), repositioned under the bonnet on the left-hand inner wing, served the newly-introduced dual-circuit braking system. To release the bonnet catch, the pull knob remained under the dashboard on the left-hand side (far left, centre), a constant source of irritation to the owners of right-hand drive cars. The rear view mirror (far left, bottom) was now very much larger than at any time in the Beetle's history, and was designed to detach from its mounting upon impact.

A conventional straight gear lever but no clutch. The advantage of the semi-automatic cars lies less with the transmission and more with the layout of the rear suspension, which became fully independent with diagonal trailing arms and jointed driveshafts. Manual Beetles retained conventional swing axles. This layout of two heater control levers either side of the handbrake had been introduced in 1964, although the knobs were red and grey on earlier cars.

ified, a '12-volt' sticker coloured red and silver was applied to the bodywork below the A-post on the left-hand side.

Except on the 1200, dual-circuit brakes replaced the older single-circuit system, and the white plastic fluid reservoir was now placed on the inside of the left-hand front inner wing.

The 1500 became available with semi-automatic transmission (and the 1300 followed in 1968), which worked on a similar principle to the system fitted to the equally unloved Sportomatic version of the Porsche 911. As fitted to the Beetle, there was a three-speed gearbox (with ratios corresponding to second, third and fourth on the manual cars), a conventional clutch and a torque converter. The system was not fully automatic because you still had to use the gear lever to change up and down, but pneumatic operation of the clutch dispensed with the

need for a clutch pedal. A vacuum control valve on the left-hand side of the engine bay was operated by a solenoid which engaged a switch at the bottom of the gear lever, allowing you to change gear simply by moving the lever. The idea worked well enough, but both performance and fuel consumption suffered.

The great advantage of the semi-automatic cars has less to do with the transmission than it has with the revised layout of the rear swing-axles which were double-jointed (à la Porsche) and no longer contained within tubes. Under hard cornering, these double-jointed axles curtailed the tendency of the Beetle to tuck under a rear wheel, which was not only safer but allowed an enthusiastic driver to conduct his car through the corners a good deal faster – in theory anyhow. Today, the semi-auto cars are rare but the passage of time has done little to increase their desirability.

Although the basic style of the dashboard remained unchanged, safety dictated that the various control knobs were made of soft plastic, were flatter in shape, and were marked according to their function.

A particularly welcome modification was the repositioning of the ignition switch (right), which was integrated into the steering column. Arguably the best improvement made to the post-1967 cars was the 12-volt electrical system powered by a large Bosch battery housed, as usual, under the rear seat on the right-hand side (far right).

PRODUCTION CHANGES
1967

117 674 559 (Apr)
Upper part of 30 PICT carburettor fitted with thicker throttle valve spindle with two shims (previously without shims).

118 000 001 (Aug)
Headlamps mounted vertically and profile of front wings modified to suit; tail lights enlarged; bumpers larger, stronger and higher, requiring changes to bonnet and engine lids; horn grilles discontinued (except on 1200); rubber covers on running boards no longer colour-matched, always black; new fresh air ventilation system with air intake louvres at back of bonnet; external door handles with triggers; fuel tank filler neck accessible through flap in right-hand front inner wing (previously under bonnet); control knobs flat shaped with symbols denoting function; water bottle for wind-screen washer mounted behind spare wheel, with compressed air taken from spare wheel; wiper shaft spigot increased from 5mm to 7mm diameter; ignition switch mounted on steering column; fuel gauge built in to speedometer; electrical system increased from 6-volt 66Ah to 12-volt 36Ah; speedometer secured with a circlip (previously split-pin); steering column with expanded steel collapsible safety tube; dual-circuit brakes introduced (except on 1200).

118 000 002 (Aug)
Tail pipes reduced in length from 276mm to 249mm. Rear brake shoes increased from 30mm to 40mm.

118 000 003 (Aug)
1500 engine 30 PICT/2 carburettor fitted with larger float chamber.

118 233 162 (Oct)
Intake air pre-heating with thermostat regulation.

118 431 161 (Dec)
Breather pipe for fuel tank now inside fuel tank. Previously ran across top of petrol tank from filler.

1968

Volkswagen went through something of a difficult period during 1968. Heinz Nordhoff, who had successfully remained at the helm of the company since 1948, died on 12 April aged 69, his place being taken by Kurt Lotz. Yet despite the management transition and despite press criticism that the Beetle was long overdue for replacement, Volkswagen of America enjoyed record sales of 399,674 cars for the year, a figure that would not be beaten. Total Beetle production for 1968 exceeded 1.1 million and increased to over 1.2 million in 1969, figures which offer conclusive proof that commentators who continued to knock the Beetle did so out of a sense of wishful thinking. The Beetle, especially the 1500 and the later 1600, was a refined, even sophisticated, vehicle which the world's car-buying public still wanted in increasing numbers. Outwardly, the 1500 and 1300 models remained much the same, but detail changes continued to be made in 1968.

For security reasons, the bonnet release, previously a pull knob on the left beneath the dashboard, became a handle in the glovebox. This was a great improvement, particularly for the drivers of right-hand-drive cars who were well and truly fed up with having to reach into the passenger footwell merely to open the bonnet. Incidentally, the screws which secure the bonnet handle in the glovebox have a tendency to work loose with prolonged use, so a couple of minutes with a screwdriver to tighten them up is time well spent. Do not wait until the screws become so loose that the glovebox rattles around in limbo, because this situation not only makes it extremely difficult to release the bonnet catch, but will usually result in the contents of your glovebox emptying themselves in the boot compartment.

The petrol filler flap was now lockable, not with a key but by a cable-operated metal catch released by pulling a plastic ring handle built into the inside of the front inner wing on the right-hand side. This is a wonderfully simple system, but the ring handle has an irritating tendency to snap off as it weakens with age and will inevitably let you down when you are completely out of petrol in the middle of nowhere. Happily, replacement handles are available from main dealers and I would like to take this opportunity to wish you the very best of luck in fitting one.

The front heating vents in the sills were moved a few inches back beneath the door openings, and the volume of air passing through them was controlled, for this model year only, by remote levers, one at the top of each footwell side. Hazard warning lights, a particularly novel feature in 1968, were fitted, and operated by a knob on the dashboard containing a red plastic lens in the centre. But by far the most bewildering alteration for the 1969 model year was the application of a decal on the ashtray depicting the gearchange pattern. The familiar 'H' pattern had

never been changed, so it remains a mystery why Volkswagen deemed it necessary suddenly to start explaining how to change gear.

From August, the 1300 was available with semi-automatic transmission, although in practice very few people took the company up on its offer, and with optional disc brakes. Cars destined for North America fitted with a manual gearbox became available with the double-jointed rear axle, which caused consternation among German customers who had to be content with the more conventional and less satisfactory rear suspension layout.

PRODUCTION CHANGES 1968

118 435 461 (Jan)
Corrosion-prevention for engine studs; parts of cylinder heads coated with a clear varnish.

118 443 379 (Jan)
Hazard warning lights introduced.

118 516 995 (Jan)
Fuel put in cars at the factory contains anti-corrosion agent.

118 799 673 (May)
All engines provided with sticker on fan housing for ignition setting; text on batteries in German, English and French; rocker cover gaskets made of compressed cork (previously of Flexolit).

118 857 240 (May)
Steering knuckle: inner taper roller bearing seat increased from 27mm to 29mm. Track rod end spigot increased from 12mm to 14mm.

119 000 001 (Aug)
Lockable petrol filler flap operated by cable pull; bonnet release moved into glove compartment; front heating vents moved back to beneath the door openings and controlled by remote levers on footwell sides.

119 000 002 (Aug)
1300 available with front disc brakes.

119 000 008 (Aug)
1300 available with semi-automatic transmission. Double-jointed rear suspension available in the USA with manual gearbox.

COLOURS

From August 1968
Royal Red
Chinchilla
Toga White
Cobalt Blue
Diamond Blue
Peru Green
Savanna Beige
Black
Yukon Yellow
Poppy Red

One small August 1968 modification that was particularly welcomed on right-hand drive cars was the repositioning of the bonnet release handle in the glovebox.

Between its launch in 1967 and 1970, modifications to the 1300 and 1500 12-volt cars were in the nature of small refinements, the cars remaining the same except in detail. Julie Kaye's 1300 is interesting: although it was built in September 1969 (the 1970 model year), it retains a number of features, including black and cream wheels, that belong in the 1969 model year.

Although the gearchange pattern had never altered, Volkswagen bewilderingly introduced a transfer on the ashtray indicating where each 'cog' could be found.

A new ring pull below the dashboard (right) released the petrol filler flap, while the handle below, which lasted only for the 1969 model year, controlled the heater vent in the sills. A similar control handle was fitted on the other side of the car. Whereas the heater vents were previously situated in the front footwells, they were moved along the sills in August 1968 to a new position close to the front of the seats (far right).

1969

With production continuing at a frantic pace, the company, in order to broaden the Beetle's appeal further, offered the 1300 and 1500 (but not the 1200) with an optional 'luxury' package which was particularly welcomed in the US and European markets, but in Britain the extra cost deterred the majority of customers, who were content to stick with the familiar package.

The luxury Beetle, distinguished externally by an 'L' badge on the engine lid, had a host of features which would be taken for granted on today's cars. Built-in reversing lights (which were optional anyway), an anti-dazzle rear view mirror, a padded dashboard in black vinyl, rubber inserts embedded in the bumpers, a lockable glovebox lid and special deep-pile carpets were all part of the package. Laudable as this move was, Volkswagen was finding it increasingly difficult to camouflage the fact that the classic torsion-bar Beetles were rapidly reaching the end of their development.

Volkswagen's most powerful Beetle, the 1500, came with a louvred engine lid for the 1970 model year. The saloon gained 10 louvres in two banks of five, whereas the cabriolet version had 28 in four banks of seven. The modification proved a more significant advantage on the cabriolet: since the rag-top lacked the row of vents below the rear window found on its tin-top sisters, its engine needed all the cool air it could get, especially when driven with the hood down. As a result of this change, a water drainage tray in black-painted steel was bolted to the underside of the engine lid.

American-specification cars were slightly different from those sold in Europe, and included a buzzer device to warn the driver in the event of a door not being secured properly. The cabriolet also had an engine transplant in the form of the 1600 Transporter unit, but British and European customers would have to wait another year before they too could buy a 1600 Beetle.

Inside the car, the Beetle lost its dashboard moulding strips and the hot air vents in the sills were fitted with small sliding covers which most people found they could operate with their feet.

The pre-heating system fitted to the 1500 engine found its way on to both the 1200 and 1300 models. At the same time, the oilways in all power units were enlarged to improve lubrication.

All Beetles for the 1970 model year had their road wheels painted silver, whereas previously they had black centres and cream rims. Although hardly an improvement aesthetically, the silver wheels are at least a good deal easier to repaint after shotblasting. Incidentally, even with the most powerful shotblasting equipment, it is virtually impossible to remove all the rust that inevitably forms in the deep crevice between the rim and the hub, and in cases of advanced corrosion a new set of wheels is probably

your best bet. Beetle wheels are immensely strong, well-made and rarely prone to breaking because of rust, but common sense surely dictates that a weakened set is a potential menace on the road.

For many, the 1970 model year represents the end of a classic era and, in the 1500, the ultimate development of the torsion-bar cars, notwithstanding the limited edition GT model launched in 1972. From here on, everything would be very different indeed.

Cars equipped with the luxury package were appropriately badged. The white patch is the edge of this Belgian-registered car's nationality plate.

Whereas the single-port 1300s had a plain engine lid, that of the 1500 gained two banks of five louvres to improve engine cooling. When the 1300 was fitted with twin-port cylinder heads for the 1971 model year, it too had the same number of louvres cut into the lid.

Rubber bumper inserts and reversing lights were part of the luxury package.

CHASSIS DATING	
Jan	119 565 362
Feb	119 653 984
Mar	119 753 726
Apr	119 852 530
May	119 942 556
Jun	119 1 040 194
Jul	119 1 093 704
Aug	110 2 092 844
Sep	110 2 191 729
Oct	110 2 300 599
Nov	110 2 395 272
Dec	110 2 473 153

For the 1970 model year, both the 1300 and 1500 were available with an optional 'L' (Luxury) package. Pascal Knockaert's 1300L was originally owned by his grandfather and has covered less than 40,000km since new. The attractive Lemmerz wheels are genuine German accessories, but were not offered by Volkswagen as part of the luxury package.

The all-original vinyl seats and interior panels in Pascal Knockaert's Beetle are colour-coded to the paintwork.

PRODUCTION CHANGES
1969

110 2 000 001 (Aug)
Optional 'L' (luxury) package introduced for 1300 and 1500 models (but not the 1200); dashboard moulding strip discontinued; road wheels now painted silver; speedometer casing no longer chromed but matt finish;
pre-heating of carburettor by hot air from left cylinder head transferred to right head.

110 2 000 002 (Aug)
Solex 30 PICT/2 carburettor fitted with additional mixture screw.

110 2 000 003 (Aug)
Engine lid on 1500 fitted with air louvres in two banks of five.

The heater vents, which had moved to this position below the door openings in August 1968, were now operated by short handles.

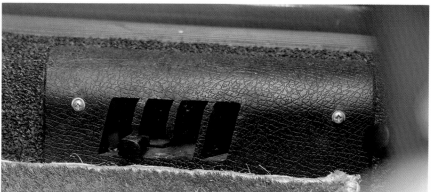

An attractive padded dashboard in black vinyl was a most worthwhile part of the luxury package. The unattractive steering wheel glove and modern radio are afterthoughts.

Following the 1500 of the previous year, the 1200 and 1300 engines benefited from the pre-heated air for the carburettor being thermostatically controlled.

COLOURS

From August 1969
Pastel White
Cobalt Blue
Royal Red
Chinchilla
Savanna Beige
Elm Green
Black
Clementine
Diamond Blue
Yukon Yellow
Poppy Red
Deep Sea Green

1970

Apart from the new 50bhp 1600 twin-port engine fitted to the 1302S, the rear suspension became fully independent with a layout similar to that of the semi-automatic Beetle introduced three years earlier, and MacPherson struts replaced torsion bars at the front.

Although the 1200 and 1300 torsion-bar Beetles continued in production, the 1500 was sadly dropped from the range and a completely new Beetle was launched in the form of the 1302 range, powered by a 1300 engine in 44bhp form or a 1600 engine with 50bhp. In terms of design philosophy, this represented the most radical ever departure from Porsche's original car. The rugged torsion bar suspension at the front was scrapped in favour of MacPherson struts, while at the rear the double-jointed axle, first seen on the semi-automatic cars three years previously, was fitted as standard equipment, except on the basic 1200 and 1300 models. The 'entry-level' 1200, incidentally, retained its traditional torsion bar layout right up to its demise in 1978.

Because Volkswagen continued to make a 1300 torsion bar Beetle, the new MacPherson strut cars might logically have received a 1301 badge, but that number was already used by Simca for one of its now very rare saloon models. So Volkswagen instead adopted the 1302 appellation, which was reasonably logical except for the fact that the 1600 version became a 1302S, which was not logical at all.

Sophisticated and considerably more complex than the classic Beetles of yesteryear, the strut cars met with a mixed reaction from press and enthusiasts alike. Somehow, the Beetle was not the same. Yes, the 1302 still looked like a proper VW except for the revised and pregnant-looking front end, and the roadholding (but not the handling) was arguably improved. All things considered, however, the new chassis, heavily influenced by and similar in layout to Volkswagen's Type 4 launched in 1968, just did not belong to the Beetle.

Road & Track magazine described the new 'Super Beetle' as, 'The best yet but still not as good as the competition'. The magazine's road test concluded: 'The Beetle, whether in standard or Super form, has three main points to recommend it: fuel economy, workmanship and its reputation for long life and good service. If you value these three virtues above all others, then the Beetle is for you. Otherwise, it is hopelessly outdated and outdone by both Japanese and American economy cars.'

Following the similar practice adopted by many other manufacturers, the MacPherson strut, with its integral damper and coil spring, is located at the top in a turret built into the front inner wing and at the bottom at the steering balljoint, with the result that the strut, framehead and radius arm all conspire to form a strong triangular structure. The large anti-roll bar or stabiliser bar attached to the framehead also acts as a location point for the two struts and is burdened by the inherent loads imposed under braking.

Generally, the strut cars are more expensive to restore than torsion bar Beetles. If you are considering buying a 1302 or 1302S, it is important to check carefully the condition of the metalwork to which the suspension is attached, particularly at the top of the front inner wings. The underside of the spare wheel well can also rot with a vengeance and replacing this panel is neither easy nor cheap.

Fitting MacPherson struts at the front allowed the luggage space under the bonnet to be increased by an incredible 85 per cent. Instead of being upright, the spare wheel was placed horizontally at the base of the luggage bay, and the fuel tank was consequently moved back. To accommodate the new suspension layout, the bonnet, front valance and wings were reshaped, and all models in the range (except the 1200) were fitted with crescent-shaped air vents behind the rear side windows. Because the large body panel in which the vents were placed was common to all Beetles, the 1200 came with a blank indentation also in the shape of a crescent. The bumper brackets were also strengthened and the rear-left included an integral towing bracket.

No radical changes were made to the interior for the time being, but the jack was placed near the battery under the rear seat, necessitating the removal of rear passengers in the event of a puncture – a famous backward step. Inside the cabin, two fresh air vents on either side of the back window corresponded to the crescent-shaped vents on the outside of the car.

The 1300 engine and the newly-introduced 1600 unit had revised cylinder heads with two inlet ports per head for more efficient 'breathing'. The twin-port engines are easily distinguishable from the single-port units by the revised inlet manifold, which has two separate pipes at each end beautifully cast in aluminium alloy and bolted to each cylinder head. Strong rubber gaskets were used to seal the pipes to the main branches of the manifold.

The result of this modification, which the specialist tuning company, Okrasa, had been offering as part of a tuning kit for many years and which Volkswagen already employed on other models in its range, was a modest but worthwhile increase in power. In the case of the 1300 engine, power was up from 40bhp to 44bhp (the same as the single-port 1500 engine). The 1302S model's new 1600 engine, displacing 1584cc thanks to the bore increasing by 2.5mm to 85.5mm, delivered an honest 50bhp. The 1200 continued with single-port heads and 34bhp. As far as choice was concerned, potential Beetle owners could not have been better served.

Other engine modifications included a more efficient oil cooler, which was made from aluminium instead of steel and was relocated slightly further for-

The new 1302 model marked a radical departure from the classic designs of previous years. Although the rear styling was not altered, the front received a longer bonnet and reshaped wings. This splendid 1302S, which belongs to Gordon Sellars, is fitted with optional bumper overriders and attractive alloy wheel trims.

TECHNICAL OUTLINES

1300 (twin-port)
Cubic capacity
1285cc
Bore and stroke
77×69mm
Compression ratio
7.5:1
Carburettor Solex 31 PICT 4
Max power 44bhp at 4100rpm
Gear ratios
1st   3.78:1
2nd   2.06:1
3rd   1.26:1
4th   0.93:1
Reverse 3.79:1
Final drive ratio
4.375:1

1600 (twin-port)
Cubic capacity
1584cc
Bore and stroke
85.5×69mm
Compression ratio
7.5:1
Carburettor Solex 34 PICT 3
Max power 50bhp at 4000rpm
Gear ratios
1st   3.78:1
2nd   2.06:1
3rd   1.26:1
4th   0.93:1
Reverse 3.79:1
Final drive ratio
3.875:1

Crescent-shaped fresh air vents (far left) appeared behind the rear side windows on all models except the 1200, which had a blank indentation. The engine lid of the 1302S (left) is identical to that of the 1500 model, which was dropped from the range in July 1970. The 'S' designation differentiated the 1600 version.

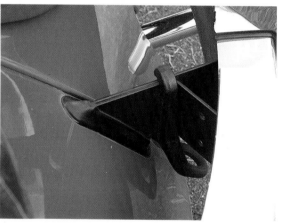

A useful towing hook (far left) was fitted to the left-hand rear bumper hanger from August 1970. Thanks to MacPherson struts, luggage space under the bonnet (left) increased by a remarkable 85 per cent, silencing for good all the critics who had complained that it was impossible to get little more than a couple of squashy bags into the torsion bar Beetles.

Instead of being held in an upright position, the spare wheel (far left) on the MacPherson strut cars was located horizontally in a sunken well. With the jack (left) now housed under the rear seat, a puncture meant persuading rear passengers to vacate their positions, not easy on a cold, wet night! The chassis number, as ever, is visible on the central tunnel.

ward on the crankcase to take greater advantage of cooling air from the fan.

With the benefit of hindsight, it is easy to sit back and criticise the twin-port engines, which became notorious for utterly appalling flat-spots and for cracking their cylinder heads. To address the need for more power, Volkswagen simply bored an additional hole in each head – the alternative was the expense of designing a completely new engine. As an aside, the demands of rebellious Ethiopian soldiers for more pay and improved working conditions led, among other things, to the downfall in 1974 of

Emperor Haile Selassie, the self-styled dictator who escaped from the marauding mob not in a blaze of glory, but in a Marina Blue 1300 twin-port Beetle that by all accounts was about the only reliable weapon left in his armoury. The fact that Selassie's escape was successful presumably means that the engine's head was not cracked, unlike his own.

As usual, all-round drum brakes were standard on both the 1200 and 1300 torsion bar cars, but front discs were an optional extra on the 1302 model. Both the 1302S 1600 saloon and cabriolet were fitted with front discs as standard equipment.

The dashboard of the 1302S remained unchanged except that bright trim was no longer applied across the width of the panel, having been discontinued on the last of the 1500 models. The owner has fitted auxiliary items beneath the radio and ashtray.

The new 1600 engine delivered 6bhp more than the 1500, thanks to the increase in capacity and the adoption of twin-port cylinder heads, which allowed the unit to breath more efficiently.

COLOURS

From August 1970
Pastel White
Clementine
Marina Blue
Kansas Beige
Sapphire Blue
Elm Green
Black
Iberian Red
Deep Sea Green
Shantung Yellow
Silver Metallic
Colorado Metallic
Gemini Metallic

PRODUCTION CHANGES
1970

110 2 528 697 (Jan)
Clamps holding petrol tank in place have rounded edges, previously square.

111 2 000 002 (Aug)
Front end of bodywork revised, including bonnet, to accommodate MacPherson strut suspension; engine changes as described in text; jack now sited below rear seat; stronger bumper brackets with integral towing bracket at rear left; crescent-shaped ventilation louvres introduced behind rear side windows but not on 1200; thermostat fitted to air cleaner. 1302S fitted with front disc brakes to the same size and specification as the 1500, backing plates modified. Front drums on 1302 (with 1200 or 1300 engine) increased in diameter to 248mm and shoe width to 45mm. Rear drums remain unchanged.

111 2 000 003 (Aug)
Crankcase halves made from better quality and more heat-resistant alloy.

111 2 325 213 (Nov)
Front torsion bar beam fitted with towing eye, on torsion bar 1200/1300 models.

1971

Purists are often heard to argue that although the Beetles manufactured from here on were more powerful and more sophisticated, quality generally declined despite the fact that quality control at the factory remained as stringent as ever. Take a look at almost any average Beetle from the early to mid 1970s and it will often be a fairly sorry sight. Typically, but not in all cases, it will have been consumed by rust to an extent previously unknown with Beetles, but in this respect Volkswagen's products were far from unique. The 1970s was an era in which the cars from most European and Japanese manufacturers suffered unusually badly from 'tin worm', for reasons that will probably never be known.

Modifications for the 1972 model year were confined to detail. The bodywork remained virtually the same apart from the saloon's rear window increasing in height by 4cm and the engine lid gaining additional louvres on all models except the 1200 (which did not need them) and the cabriolet (which had them anyway). Whereas the saloon previously had two banks of five louvres, the new lid had two banks of seven on the far left and right and two banks of six in the middle, making a total of 26 louvres altogether. The water drainage tray on the underside was

discontinued, however, with the inevitable result that the bottom inch or two of the lid would, given time, turn from a nicely-sculpted piece of pressed German steel into a rather ugly piece of German rust – just one example of how quality began to decline.

Inside the car, the number of vents either side of the rear window was increased from two to three on each side to improve interior ventilation, but the most obvious feature for the 1972 model year was the arrival of a new four-spoke steering wheel similar to the one employed on the Porsche 911 and VW Porsche 914. Designed to reduce the risk of the driver suffering serious chest injuries in the event of a collision, the wheel had a flat centre (which also served as the horn button) of soft plastic, in the middle of which was an impression of the Wolfsburg crest. The new steering wheel, which was not fitted to the 1200, was very modern and pleasant to use, but the dashboard was the same as ever. In the absence of a padded dash being specified, the two together looked incongruous. At the same time, the windscreen wiper/washer switch was transferred from a button on the dashboard to a stalk on the right-hand side of the steering column.

To bring the Beetle right up to date, the engine

One of Volkswagen's finest achievements occurred in February 1972 when production reached 15,007,034, surpassing the Ford Model T's world record. To celebrate this milestone, a special edition 'Marathon' or 'World Champion' Beetle was launched. Based on a 1300 torsion bar car, the Marathon received special light metallic blue paintwork and 10-spoke wheels. Among the 1971 changes illustrated by this car, owned from new by Vic Kaye, are the enlarged rear window (height increased by 4cm) and the engine lid's additional louvres, embellished here by period bright trims.

In keeping with regular non-1200 Beetles for the 1972 model year, the Marathon (right) is fitted with a four-spoke safety steering wheel. Note the commemorative 'World Champion' glovebox plaque, which was issued to all Marathon owners.

CHASSIS DATING

Jan	111 2 518 856
Feb	111 2 669 687
Mar	111 2 730 614
Apr	111 2 832 863
May	111 2 932 741
Jun	111 3 034 569
Jul	111 3 143 119
Aug	112 2 067 069
Sep	112 2 124 590
Oct	112 2 299 678
Nov	112 2 356 908
Dec	112 2 427 792

Upholstery was typically in black vinyl during the early 1970s. For the 1972 model year, there was an additional vent – an increase from two to three – on each side of the rear window.

The significant difference in the 1300 engine compartment was a reshaped air filter fitted with vacuum and temperature controlled pre-heating. This one-owner car is impossible to fault for originality.

1972

An additional stalk was fitted to the steering column for the windscreen wiper and washer function.

For ease of servicing, an electronic diagnostic socket was fitted in the top left of the engine compartment.

was fitted with an electronic diagnosis connection which, when plugged in to a dealer's computerised machine, was capable of discovering a number of fundamental faults. At this stage, major servicing, which was recommended at 6000 miles or six-month intervals, covered a check on no fewer than 88 different components or functions including, for example, compression testing on all four cylinders, dynamo current and even the torque of the wheel bolts. Incidentally, several 1300 and 1600 Beetles at around this time escaped from the factory with a sticker on the fan housing recommending that the valve clearances be set to 0.004in. If your car retains one of these stickers, you may like to keep it for the sake of originality and as a reassuring reminder that even Volkswagen occasionally makes mistakes – the clearances should be set at 0.006in.

Volkswagen had its most successful year ever, producing 1,291,612 Beetles world-wide in 1971.

PRODUCTION CHANGES
1971

111 2 920 875 (Jun)
Double vacuum distributor modified to single vacuum; retard take-off for ignition timing discontinued on Solex 30, 31 and 34 PICT/3 carburettors, but not for cars destined for North America.

112 2 000 001 (Aug)
Height of rear window increased by 4cm; revised engine lid with two banks of seven louvres and two banks of six.

112 2 000 002 (Aug)
Windscreen wiper switch transferred from dashboard to stalk on right-hand side of the steering column.

122 2 000 009 (Aug)
Exhaust gas recirculation system added for cars to California.

112 2 073 652 (Sep)
Clutch operating arm lengthened and smoother in use.

The company reached a motoring milestone on 17 February when production passed 15,007,033 units, beating the record previously set by the Ford Model T and making the Beetle the best-selling car of all time. More recently, the factory in Mexico celebrated the production of the 21 millionth Beetle – a record that will surely stand for all time?

The actual car that broke the Model T's produc-

Exclusive to Britain, the limited edition GT was based on the 1300 torsion bar car, but fitted with the 1600 engine. Sports wheels were among several special features. This apple green example is owned by John Alexander.

tion record was a 1302S, but the car launched to mark the occasion was, paradoxically, a traditional torsion bar car. A special edition, the 'World Champion' or 'Marathon' Beetle was a 1300, with metallic blue paintwork and 10-spoke sports wheels that were said to have been inspired, perhaps fancifully, by the Model T's artillery wheels.

During the same year, Britain celebrated the import of its 300,000th Beetle and also launched a special edition badged as a 'GT'. Available exclusively in Britain, the GT was painted apple green, tomato red or lemon yellow, the latter being by far the most common. The 2500 GT Beetles made were based on the 1300 torsion bar car, but came equipped with the more powerful 50bhp 1600 engine. Apart from colour, the car is recognisable externally by a GT badge on the engine lid (although some GTs were badged 1300S just to con-

Instead of vinyl, the GT's seats were in comfortable cloth material and were mounted on a 'safety' pyramid structure, a feature shared with the 1303.

In place of the traditional oil bath air cleaner, the 1600 engine had a dry paper element inside an enlarged plastic casing.

fuse matters), 4½J sports wheels and the very large rear lights fitted to the 1303 launched in August. Internally, there was a padded dashboard, a wooden gear knob and special latticework decoration on the gear lever, while the comfortable seats were mounted on a new triangular safety frame also fitted to the 1303.

Today, the GT is particularly sought-after not just because it was a special edition but also because, from a driver's point of view, it is undoubtedly one of the finest Beetles ever made, a truly worthy successor to the 1500 in most respects. The GT retained the wonderful handling characteristics of the good old swing-axle cars, while the 1600 engine really allowed an enthusiastic driver to get a move on,

especially as the power enabled the GT to be steered on the throttle through bends. For reasons best-known to criminologists, psychologists and masters of primitive human behaviour, the GT engine lid badges are also highly-prized pieces of merchandise, collected by people who are sufficiently rich to afford a screwdriver but seemingly too impecunious to fund their insatiable desire to own trivial pieces of automobilia, and therefore taking what the law recognises as belonging to others.

The 1973 model year saw another major facelift with the launch in August of the 1303, a car with modifications that marked 'the beginning of the end' in the development of the Beetle. The 1303 was a logical progression from the earlier 1302 Beetles in

CHASSIS DATING	
Jan	112 2 482 841
Feb	112 2 583 722
Mar	112 2 679 613
Apr	112 2 772 211
May	112 2 859 409
Jun	112 2 951 706
Jul	112 2 961 362
Aug	113 2 115 694
Sep	113 2 199 639
Oct	113 2 287 110
Nov	113 2 372 878
Dec	113 2 438 833

All GT Beetles came with a padded dashboard, four-spoke safety steering wheel and a gear lever with a polished wooden knob and a special lattice pattern.

The 1303 received a totally different padded dashboard with fresh air ventilation across the whole width and swivel flaps on the far left and right. The speedometer was housed in a high plastic shroud and the fusebox was now in the centre under the dashboard.

The GT shared its 'elephantine' rear lights with the 1303 launched in August 1972, and carried a GT badge.

that it inherited MacPherson struts up front and double-jointed axles at the rear, but there were, once again, significant modifications to the bodywork. If the Beetle-buying public had by now accepted the pregnant front end of the 1302 and 1302S, Volkswagen had another shock in store when it introduced the big bulbous windscreen, which necessitated shortening the top of the bonnet. Enlarging the windscreen by 42 per cent improved forward vision still further and helped the car's aerodynamic properties, but it arguably did nothing to enhance the appearance of the Beetle.

At the same time, the V-over-W emblem at the top of the bonnet was discontinued and the push button incorporated into the bonnet handle was made of black plastic. The rear wings were more bulbous, having been reshaped for the purpose of fitting much larger rear lights, and an additional piece of grooved brightwork was added to both sides of the lengthened front bulkhead or scuttle.

Not for the first time in its career, the dashboard underwent a complete transformation to make it more in keeping with the modern automobile age. Gone was the classic but austere metal dash of the previous years and in its place came an attractive plastic moulded affair. To sound a negative note, the glovebox lid could no longer double as a tea tray when opened, since it now rested at an angle. Fresh-air vents with swivel flaps were placed on both sides of the dashboard, and the speedometer, with its inte-

gral fuel gauge and warning lights, sat high up in a plastic shroud.

For safety reasons, the front seats were mounted on steel pyramid structures welded directly to the floorpan. Because this arrangement allowed for greater seat adjustment, both the gear lever and handbrake were moved backward. The seats were adjustable fore and aft with handles mounted on either side of the central backbone, rather than in front of the seat frames as previously.

Both the 1300 and 1600 twin-port engines were available in the 1303 model, the 1600 version following familiar practice in being badged a 1303S. The most visible alteration was a new air filter, a large plastic box which was fitted with a conventional paper filter instead of being filled with a small quantity of oil. Easier to change and costing a little more than oil, the paper element had the distinct advantage of being a good deal less messy. For traditionalists, the single-port 1200 Beetle was still fitted with the ubiquitous oil bath filter.

PRODUCTION CHANGES
1972

113 2 000 003 (Aug)
Coil spring clutch replaced by diaphragm spring clutch.

113 2 000 004 (Aug)
Curved windscreen 1303 launched with revised bodywork; bonnet made shorter to accommodate panoramic windscreen; V-over-W badge on bonnet discontinued; black plastic push button on bonnet handle; modern moulded dashboard introduced on 1303 with speedometer contained in shroud; seats mounted on safety-inspired pyramid structure; windscreen wipers modified to fit new windscreen.

133 2 000 011 (Aug)
Fusebox relocated below the centre of the dashboard on new 1303.

113 2 196 230 (Sep)
New thermostat for accelerator pump on 31 PICT/4 carburettor; oil bath air cleaner replaced by large plastic box with dry paper element.

113 2 362 151 (Nov)
30 PICT/3 carburettor fitted with foam float.

Announced in August 1972, the 1303 and 1303S were heavily revised versions of the 1302 MacPherson strut cars. Although most of the visible changes were at the front, larger rear lights were mounted on modified wings. Roger Slim's 'Big' Beetle is a limited edition 1600 which was offered in 1973. These attractive 5½J wheels were Volkswagen accessories which were standard on the 'Big' Beetle.

In order to accommodate a revised 'safety' dashboard, the 1303 and 1303S models had a panoramic windscreen, a shorter and more bulbous bonnet, and a longer scuttle. A short piece of grooved brightwork adorned both sides of the scuttle, the bonnet handle had a black plastic push button, and the VW bonnet emblem was discontinued.

The 1303 glovebox was divided into separate compartments, but the fact that the lid no longer opened flat meant a useful practical feature had been lost.

COLOURS

From August 1972
Pastel White
Brilliant Orange
Texas Yellow
Marina Blue
Kasan Red
Black
Sumatra Green
Biscay Blue
Kansas Beige
Maya Metallic
Alaska Metallic
Turquoise Metallic
Marathon Metallic

1973

CHASSIS
DATING

Jan	113 2 524 536
Feb	113 2 606 864
Mar	113 2 705 303
Apr	113 2 787 815
May	113 2 883 926
Jun	113 2 978 660
Jul	113 3 021 911
Aug	114 2 135 126
Sep	114 2 175 197
Oct	114 2 264 932
Nov	114 2 356 316
Dec	114 2 423 795

Based on the 1200, the Jeans Beetle differed in specification from market to market. With denim seats, bright paintwork, matt black trim and sports wheels, it was aimed at fashionable but impecunious youngsters, and around 50,000 were made.

With the industrialised world rocked by a major oil crisis, Volkswagen, along with the majority of European car producers, strove to design new models that were more economical and utilised petrol more efficiently. The Beetle range was as comprehensively wide as it possibly could be with the basic 1200 offering 'no frills' motoring at entry level and the 1600 cabriolet providing fun and luxury at the top end of the scale, but the launch of the front-engined, front-wheel drive, water-cooled Golf was just 12 months away and meant that the end of the road – in Wolfsburg at least – was at last in sight for the Beetle.

The creation of further special editions helped to rejuvenate the Beetle's flagging appeal. By far the most prolific special edition was the 'Jeans' model, which was aimed principally at impecunious younger people, with its bright yellow paintwork and blue denim seats. Based on the 34bhp 1200, the Jeans was distinguished externally by attractive 4½J sports wheels (similar to those fitted to the GT model in Britain the previous year) and by black plastic stripes along the bottom of the doors which were continued across the rear quarter panels and incorporated the word Jeans also in black plastic. An additional Jeans motif appeared on the engine lid. The headlight rims were in matt black, the bumpers were matt black with a chrome strip in the central groove, and the body mouldings were in black anodised aluminium alloy. Also in black were the bonnet and engine lid handles, while the window rubbers were devoid of bright trim.

Between September 1973 and late 1975, some

50,000 Jeans Beetles were made and they varied in specification from one market to another. In Europe, there were red, blue and orange versions, the latter being the best equipped of all as it came with integral headrests, a heated rear window, a padded dashboard, halogen headlight bulbs and rear fog lights. Volkswagen's South African factory also made a Jeans Beetle, but its version had bolder Jeans script applied to the doors rather than the quarter panels and the sports road wheels were to the old five-stud design and similar to the stylish wheels made in Germany

On the basic 1200 model, the headlining did not extend to the roof pillars and the grab handle mounting points above the door were crudely blanked off, but denim upholstery on the Jeans version brightened up an otherwise austere cabin.

A special edition launched in Germany in January 1973, the 'Yellow and Black Racer' was based on the 1303S and fitted with the 1600 engine.

The European-spec Jeans was fitted with standard wheels and black hubcaps. It is seen in company with the two other 1973 special editions, the 1303-based City Beetle (red) and Big Beetle (green), both of which came with attractive 5½J sports wheels.

by Lemmerz. The prototype cars, incidentally, were painted with bodywork 'stitching' to resemble a pair of jeans more closely, but mercifully this little marketing ploy was never released to the public.

Based on the 1303S, Volkswagen launched a limited edition 'Yellow and Black Racer' of which 3500 were produced from January – the bodywork was painted yellow with the bonnet and engine lid in matt black. In keeping with the *Rennsport* image, there were sports seats with integral headrests, a leather-trimmed steering wheel and 5½J sports

wheels (an attractive optional extra on the regular production cars) with 175/70×15 low-profile tyres.

Two more special editions were based on the 1303 models – the City Beetle with the 1300 engine and the Big Beetle with the 1600 unit. While the former was equipped with 4½J sports wheels, the latter came with 5½J rims – and both had a padded steering wheel, heated rear window, deep-pile carpets, reversing lights and inertia-reel seat belts.

The regular cars, meanwhile, carried on much the same as usual save that the 1200 was fitted with the rear wings, big tail lights and bumpers of the 1303 models. The bumpers on the basic 1200 were painted black (with silver paint visible in the central groove) and black anodised body mouldings were fitted, whereas the luxury version in both 1200 and 1300 forms retained fully chromed bumpers and bright polished body mouldings.

Further luxury equipment became available as options on the MacPherson strut cars which were badged 1303L and 1303LS accordingly, including cabriolet versions. All American-specification Beetles also had shock absorbers built into the bumper hangers to withstand impacts up to 5mph: in other words, they allowed you to park in tight spaces without having to worry about damage caused by bashing into the cars on either side. The 1300 and 1600 engines were both fitted with an alternator instead of a dynamo.

The most significant change on the strut cars was to the front suspension, which was modified to give negative steering roll radius rather than positive as previously. From August, the struts were shortened

1974

This was a dismal year for Beetle enthusiasts in some ways because production at Wolfsburg finally ceased on 1 July to make way for the Golf, although the Beetle continued to be made in Germany at Hanover (until 1975) and Emden. More than that, though, the 1200 torsion bar car was more basic than at almost any time in its history: when the tail pipes were painted black and the chrome-plated steel hubcaps were replaced by cheaper plastic caps that merely covered the hub nuts, the car's appearance was drab to say the least. Another penny-pinching exercise saw the removal of the glovebox lid on the 1200, although customers still had the option of having their cars fitted with the 1200 luxury package, which included a glovebox lid, padded black vinyl dashboard, chromed bumpers and bright trim around the windows.

The most clearly visible alteration for the 1975 model year was the removal of the front indicators from the top of the wings. New units were fitted into the front bumpers where they were considered to be more clearly visible to oncoming traffic, although US Beetles, with their impact bumpers, continued in production with the traditional units on top of the wings. At the rear, the number plate light pod gained a row of 19 corrugations on its top surface, although the reason for this anomalous and trivial modification is not clear.

In order to meet tougher Californian exhaust

and the flange between the strut and the steering ball joint was replaced by a clip. The centre line of control on the radius of swing of the ball joint on the modified version passed through the top of the strut and the centre of the ball joint, which had the effect of providing greater stability under braking, particularly on broken or uneven road surfaces. With the older system of positive steering roll radius, the driver had to make corrections with the steering wheel in circumstances where he experienced uneven braking, but with the modified system the uneven braking force is, in theory, completely negated. The two types of suspension are so very different that parts from one type cannot be fitted to the other.

Despite the fact that the latest Beetles were better in many respects than all those that had gone before, 1973 was the last year in which production worldwide would exceed one million units. With production falling from more than 1.2 million cars in 1973 to just over 791,000 in 1974, Volkswagen faced the real possibility of bankruptcy if a worthy replacement could not be found.

In keeping with the Jeans theme, Volkswagen mooted the application of decal 'stitching' to the bodywork, but the idea did not get beyond prototype stage…

PRODUCTION CHANGES
1973

113 2 522 922 (Jan)
Crankshaft pulley and generator pulley no longer painted black but have metallic finish.
113 2 687 765 (Mar)
Twin pre-heating tubes fitted to inlet manifold and tailbox.
133 2 802 561 (May)
Petrol filter built into fuel line replaces tank strainer.
114 2 000 001 (Aug)
MacPherson strut suspension modified to give negative steering roll radius rather than positive as previously. Sills strengthened at jacking points.
114 2 147 150 (Sep)
Solex PICT/4: vent hole fitted in accelerator pump.

COLOURS

From August 1973
Atlas White
Marine Blue
Brilliant Orange
Senegal Red
Tropical Green
Sahara Beige
Rally Yellow
Cliff Green
Black
Marathon Metallic (blue)
Alaska Metallic (blue)
Moss Metallic (green)
Metallic Beige
Tunis Yellow
Marino Yellow
Phoenix Red
Brilliant Yellow
Lofoten Green
Mandarin
Panama Green

Attractive, hard-wearing, easy-to-clean seats were in vinyl, but despite their firmness they are exceptionally supportive and comfortable on long journeys. The centre console and additional instruments are accessories.

European-spec Beetles retained a single Solex carburettor, whereas cars exported to America were by now fitted with fuel injection.

For some strange reason, the registration light pod (facing page) gained 19 corrugations along its upper surface in August 1974. In addition, the rear valance was curved instead of being flat. The tail pipes were painted black on the 1200.

emissions regulations, which would soon be extended to all US states, US cars were fitted with fuel injection and catalytic converters, which made the use of unleaded petrol mandatory. Since unleaded petrol became widely available in Europe, there has been some confusion among classic car enthusiasts as to whether older cars are eligible to run on the 'greener fuels', and where Beetles are concerned the situation remains almost, but not quite, as confused as ever. So please forgive me for expressing a personal opinion.

If your car was designed by Volkswagen specifically to accept unleaded fuel (as with those fitted with a catalytic converter), you have no option but to fill up with unleaded because leaded ruins the internal surfaces of a catalyser. Similarly, if the original cylinder heads on your car have been converted, by the fitment of special chromed valves (available from main dealers), go ahead and use unleaded. But in the case of a Beetle which has not been converted, I would suggest that you use a full-time diet of leaded petrol despite claims from a number of sources that it's perfectly safe to run on unleaded provided every fifth tankful is leaded. Many thousands of Beetle owners

in Brazil solved this problem years ago by switching to alcohol-based fuels, so perhaps one day we ought to follow their example.

Finally for the 1975 model year, the strut cars were fitted with rack and pinion steering instead of the worm and roller unit that had seen service since 1961. The new modification was a great improvement which made the steering more precise and direct, but a drawback for restorers is the fact that replacement racks, still available from main dealers at the time of writing, are extremely expensive.

PRODUCTION CHANGES 1974

115 2 000 001 (Aug)

Front bumpers fitted with indicators; rear valance modified in shape; front indicators for US cars continued on top of wings and not in bumpers; steering changed to rack and pinion. American-spec cars fitted with fuel injection, but only those destined for California also have catalytic converters. All American-spec versions received catalytic converters from the start of the 1977 model year.

The MacPherson strut saloons had a relatively short run, production ending in July 1975 after just five years. This late 1303 (above), built in February 1975, has an attractive but non-standard dealer-applied gold coachline painted on the roof, engine lid and waistline. Externally the 1303 – this example is owned by Rob Loughrey – remained much the same, but the 1975 model year version was distinguished by its front indicators, which were housed in the front bumpers instead of sitting on top of the front wings.

COLOURS

From August 1974
Atlas White
Marino Yellow
Ceylon Beige
Miami Blue
Lofoten Green
Senegal Red
Black
Rallye Yellow
Cliff Green
Phoenix Red
Marathon Blue
(metallic)
Ancona Blue (metallic)
Hellas Metallic (beige)
Viper Green (metallic)
Orange

Rectangular indicators built into the bumpers, new in 1974, are more readily visible to oncoming traffic and are still featured on the cars produced in Mexico today.

In standard form, the 1303 came with chrome-plated hub caps. This view also shows clearly the modified shape of the rear wing, to suit the large rear lights.

1975

POST-1975

With the Golf having set new standards in compact car design, sales of the Beetle declined dramatically from just under 800,000 in 1974 to fewer than 450,000 in 1975. After the demise of the MacPherson strut saloon at the end of July, the only Beetle available for the 1976 model year was the good old torsion bar car, which was available with either the 1200 single-port engine or the 1600 twin-port unit. The cabriolet, however, continued as a 1303 with strut suspension right until the end.

Despite the fact that Volkswagen was concentrating its efforts on other models, including the Polo and Passat, the little car that had contributed so much to the German economy for more than 30 years was not neglected. The 1200 version was offered with an options package that included the crescent-shaped fresh-air vents behind the rear side windows initially introduced on the 1302, chrome-plated hubcaps once again, bumpers with centrally-mounted rubber strips, and reversing lights built in to the large rear lights.

Cars bound for North America came with the option of a heated rear window, a two-speed fresh-air fan and brightwork around the windows. US cars also differed from European ones in being equipped with the double-jointed rear axle, fuel injection and a catalytic converter.

PRODUCTION CHANGES 1975

115 2 266 092 (Jul)
Last 1303 manufactured.

115 2 000 001 (Aug)
Number plate pod on 1200 gains corrugations and is made of plastic; 1200 engine fitted with paper air cleaner to replace oil bath and, at last, the 1200 is fitted with 12-volt electrics.

CHASSIS DATING	
Jan	115 2 171 603
Feb	115 2 187 424
Mar	115 2 204 329
Apr	115 2 231 711
May	115 2 248 549
Jun	115 2 259 792
Jul	115 2 266 092
Aug	116 2 004 793
Sep	116 2 041 746
Oct	116 2 047 072
Nov	116 2 060 534
Dec	116 2 071 467

COLOURS

From August 1975
Atlas White
Marino Yellow
Lofoten Green
Oceanic Blue
Senegal Red
Black
Rallye Yellow
Phoenix Red
Diamond Silver Metallic
Viper Green Metallic
Topaz Metallic

The year 1975 was most notable for the MacPherson strut saloon ceasing production in July. The MacPherson strut assembly, which lived on for cabriolet versions, was complex and required the inner wings to be very much stronger – and heavier – than those fitted to torsion bar Beetles. Front disc brakes were part of the MacPherson specification.

Through 1976 and 1977, the Beetle continued without modifications and, as production and sales declined, eventually took its final bow at the beginning of 1978. The very last German-built saloon, a 1200 with chassis number 118 2 034 030, rolled off the Emden production lines at midday on 19 January. The placard on its roof read, 'Käfer, Made in Germany 16,255,500, Production Weltweit 19,300,000'.

Even after the demise of the 1303 saloon in 1975, the cabriolet soldiered on with MacPherson strut front suspension until the end of its production run in 1980. Will Shaw's 1977 model is the perfect car for fresh air motoring.

Since 1945, each one of over 5000 components that make up every Beetle had been modified in some way or other with the exception of the clamping strips that retain the bonnet and engine lid rubber seals. German production of this truly remarkable and universally popular car ended for simple economic reasons. Volkswagen was unable to sell the Beetle in sufficient numbers to justify continuing with production, and no manufacturer can afford the luxury of sentimentality when it comes to paying the wages and preserving jobs.

The car-buying public in Europe and America demanded a great deal more from their everyday motoring needs than could be supplied by the Beetle during its twilight years. Although the Karmann-built cabriolet struggled on until 10 January 1980 (after a production run of just 332,000) mainly for the benefit of the convertible-loving American mar-

Later cabriolets are now much sought-after and command high prices. As stylish as always, these cars had come a long way since 1949 and were the most luxurious of all Beetles.

The 1977 cabriolet features adjustable head restraints on the front seats and a sumptuous interior trimmed in white vinyl to match the hood (below left). Note the position of the seat belt mounting. Double-jointed driveshafts (below), originally introduced on the semi-automatic Beetle, were fitted to all 1302 and 1303 saloons and cabriolets, and make a marked difference to the handling characteristics.

ket, the Golf quickly established itself as the People's choice for the future.

Considering the number of Beetles produced between 1945 and 1978, they are a relatively rare sight on European, British and American roads today, yet the humble Bug is more popular than ever among enthusiasts. As the years go by, more and more are being lovingly restored. But rather than being thrashed for thousands of miles, they are kept safely in a garage for occasional use in the warmer and drier months of summer.

If you are seen driving a Beetle on a daily basis in Germany, it is assumed that you are something of an eccentric and that your 'real' car is, of course, a 7-series BMW. If you drive a Beetle in Britain, you would probably love to own a 7-series BMW but most definitely not as your only car. And if you drive a Beetle in Mexico, you are probably a taxi driver

The hood still looked the same, but after 1976 the familiar heavy horsehair padding was replaced by a more modern foam material.

The padded dashboard, initially available as part of an optional 'L' package on the 1300 and 1500 in 1969, also featured on the last of the 1200 models as a 'luxury' option, along with the four-spoke steering wheel.

Since the 'entry-level' Beetle was never fitted with MacPherson struts or the revised dashboard of the 1303, the flat windscreen and regular bonnet were retained throughout (below right). Drum brakes sufficed at the front of the torsion bar car whether the 1200 or 1600 engine was fitted (below).

The 1200 was produced with a blank indentation upon the introduction of through-flow ventilation on the 1302 in 1970, but the crescent vent was added to the torsion bar car for the 1976 model year.

who does not even know or particularly care what a 7-series BMW is.

Down the years, the Beetle has been produced in Nigeria, South Africa, Mexico, Brazil, Portugal, Peru, Thailand, Costa Rica, Eire, Indonesia, Malaysia, Singapore, Belgium, the Philippines and New Zealand – as well as Germany. Production continues in Mexico at the rate of around 500 per day and production was resumed in Brazil in September 1993 due to an overwhelming demand in that country for inexpensive and economical cars.

There is even a small company, Autobarn, based near Pershore, England, specialising in the remanufacture of Beetles from 'new-old-stock' German parts and brand new components imported from Mexico. Each Beetle is entirely hand-assembled on a special jig and carries a price tag commensurate with a middle-ranking executive car, but, according to the

firm's Barbados-born managing director, Peter Stevens, the cars are to the same specification as those that would have been made by Volkswagen in Germany today had production continued. Despite the fitment of a catalytic converter, fuel injection, modern seats, tinted windows, attractive sports wheels, side impact bars in the doors and many other improvements, demand is low and production remains necessarily at a trickle. When faced with reality rather than nostalgia, the majority of people in the Western world will not buy a Beetle.

Rumours persist that it is only a matter of time before production is resumed in Germany or that Volkswagen is about to import Beetles from South America for sale in Europe. There are many technical and bureaucratic reasons why this will probably never happen, but the best reason is that the Beetle would not sell. Add that to the fact that Volkswagen

now owns Skoda, a company already making inexpensive and economical cars, and it is apparent that the Beetle no longer has a future in Europe or America, except, perhaps, in the intriguing form of the 'Concept I' Beetle revealed at the Detroit Motor Show in January 1994. Not that the Beetle will ever die completely, at least not while it remains lawful to own and drive a petrol-engined motor car. Surely the world's legislatures will have to do considerably more than pass further motoring safety and emissions laws to prevent us enjoying Beetles?

Oddly enough, no-one has arrived at a satisfactory conclusion as to the reason for the Beetle's quite extraordinary and continuing success. Rather like a clove of garlic, there is nothing startling about its individual constituents but the sum of the parts adds up to something rather useful and special. A truly 'classless' motor car, the Beetle is tough, reliable, cheap to run and maintain and is capable of enduring neglect and abuse for longer than anything else – and yet there is more. The unique styling gives the car a character which turns a lump of metal into a trustworthy friend.

Pay no attention to those who say it is ugly. I have yet to see a pretty Silver Shadow, Ford Cortina, Vauxhall Cresta, Fiat Strada, Hillman Avenger or Nissan Bluebird, but automotive beauty is of course in the eyes of the beholder. And that, for millions of people throughout the world, means a Beetle. Viewed in detail from any angle, the Beetle's bodywork is a gorgeous amalgamation of swooping curves and typically Germanic functionalism. It is pretty, yet unpretentious and thoroughly practical. That it is so very different from more conventional cars has ensured that the styling has never dated, unless you hold the view that it has always been out of date. Quite simply, the overall shape has never changed. It wouldn't be a Beetle if it had.

Throughout 1976 and 1977, the Beetle underwent very few modifications. The 1200 torsion bar car remained spartan, but was offered with the option of a 1600 engine in 1977. The 1200 had been fitted with 1303-style rear lights and wings from August 1973, and through-flow ventilation, as evidenced by the crescent-shaped vents behind the rear side windows, was specified from August 1975.

A classic car without peers. One of the last 'silver edition' Beetles imported into the UK is owned and maintained by VAG (UK) Ltd – the Volkswagen importer – and has an appropriate registration.

CHASSIS DATING 1976	
Jan	116 2 082 265
Feb	116 2 097 865
Mar	116 2 114 297
Apr	116 2 131 217
May	116 2 146 453
Jun	116 2 162 096
Jul	116 2 176 287
Aug	117 2 006 331
Sep	117 2 033 696
Oct	117 2 048 703
Nov	117 2 057 509
Dec	117 2 063 700
1977	
Jan	117 2 069 049
Feb	117 2 070 620
Mar	117 2 071 675
Apr	117 2 081 654
May	117 2 087 283
Jun	117 2 094 861
Jul	117 2 096 890
Aug	118 2 007 084
Sep	118 2 008 911
Oct	118 2 016 615
Nov	118 2 019 775
Dec	118 2 026 312
1978	
Jan	118 2 034 030
Feb	118 2 104 291
Mar	118 2 106 953
Apr	118 2 106 969
May	118 2 108 000
Jun	–
Jul	–
Aug	119 2 103 606
Sep	119 2 103 608
Oct	119 2 106 109
Nov	119 2 108 687
Dec	–

To be quite candid, Beetles are 'big business' because the little car continues to generate the kind of enthusiasm which has never been felt for any other kind of automobile. Thanks to a thriving restoration industry, rebuilding an old Beetle is an extremely attractive and worthwhile proposition. Like the Model T Ford, it is unlikely that any Beetle, with the possible exception of the cabriolet version, will ever be launched into the stratosphere where monetary values are concerned, even after a painstaking restoration. This is good news because those of us with more enthusiasm than money will always be able to afford to buy and run a Beetle.

No other car is as instantly or universally recognisable as the Beetle. No other car has made such an impact on motoring life in the 20th century, and it is unlikely that any manufacturer will ever enjoy the kind of success with one model as Volkswagen had with the Beetle. May the Beetle live for ever.

COLOURS

From August 1976	From August 1977
Panama Brown	Panama Bronze
Dakota Beige	Dakota Beige
Brocade Red	Malaga Red
Black	Black
Miami Blue	Miami Blue
Manila Green	Manila Green
Polar White	Alpine White
Riyad Yellow	Riyad Yellow
Mars Red	Mars Red
Bali Green	Bali Green
Bronze Metallic	Bronze Metallic
Viper Green Metallic	Viper Green Metallic
Diamond Silver Metallic	Diamond Silver Metallic
Timor Brown Metallic	Bahama Blue Metallic
Bahama Blue Metallic	Colibri Green Metallic

A BREATH OF FRESH AIR

Early cabriolets – this is a 1954 car – were available with two-tone paintwork, and had a small rear window and vertical cooling louvres in the engine lid.

Because Volkswagen's top brass did not envisage that demand for the expensive Beetle cabriolet, launched to the public on 1 July 1949, would be especially heavy, the whole project was farmed out to the specialist coachbuilder, Karmann, whose factory was based at Osnabrück. As it turned out, *Generaldirekteur* Heinz Nordhoff and his management were right in their assumptions because just 331,847 cabriolets were made up to January 1980, a mere drop in the ocean by comparison with the saloon.

Quite naturally, modifications made to the 'ragtop' over the years followed those of the saloon, but there were inevitably important differences between the two cars of which potential restorers should at least be aware. Remove the roof from any saloon and it soon becomes apparent where much of the body's strength lies, which is why the cabriolet's body (but not the Beetle chassis) was considerably reinforced and strengthened from the beginning.

Reinforcement panels were provided for the sills in the form of a rail on each side welded to the bottom plate of the sill, which, in section, resembles an upside-down letter 'G'. An inner strengthening panel to the rear of the front door pillars, another at the base of the B-post and further reinforcement transversely under the rear seat (which also provides a base for the seat) are other changes. The immensely strong double-skinned rear quarter panels are also substantially different in construction from those of the Beetle saloon, and obviously allow for the fact

The small rear window of the pre-1957 cars severely restricted rearward vision, but there is no doubt that these earlier cars were much cosier inside.

that the rear windows wind down. At the rear, the short panel above the engine lid is stronger than that of the saloon because it provides a mounting point for the hood, and it also lacks cooling louvres because these were transferred to the engine lid.

From the start of production, the engine lid was punctured with two banks of 18 separate vertical slots, modified in July 1957 to two banks of five louvres. Until 1951, the cabriolet's semaphore indicators were fitted to the front quarter panels, but when ventilation flaps were introduced that year, the indicators were relocated in the rear quarter panels

Cabriolets produced after July 1957 – this is a 1964 car – had a larger back window and horizontal louvres in the engine lid. By this time, single colour paint schemes were always employed.

By the 1970s, the rear window had been enlarged to keep the cabriolet in line with the saloon – and with modern driving conditions.

behind the doors, eventually being replaced altogether in August 1960 by more modern flasher units.

Until 1954, the bright trim around the side windows was of polished aluminium, whose inherent ability to tarnish quickly led to chrome-plated brass being used for the rest of production. Curiously, none of the production cabriolets ever had a split rear window, but the small oval one was increased in size for the 1958 model year, as with the saloon's rear window. In keeping with the cabriolet's very high standards of build quality, the rear window was always made of glass.

Unfortunately, many of the differences between the saloon and cabriolet are of academic interest only as early 'Split' cabriolets are extremely rare nowadays – and an even greater pity is that there are no known examples surviving in Britain. By its very design, an open-top car will, all things being equal, rot out more quickly than a tin-top. Despite the fact that the Beetle is arguably the most weatherproof cabriolet ever made, a heavy and annual dose of Waxoyl will do your car no harm at all.

As mentioned earlier, genuine Beetle cabriolets have a body badge on the right-hand front quarter panel: the badge on pre-1961 cars is rectangular and reads 'Karmann Kabriolett' with one letter 'K' sufficing for both words, whereas cars made after 1961 were fitted with a more shapely badge which simply reads 'Karmann'.

Following in the steps of the saloon, the cabriolet was available throughout the 1960s and 1970s with larger engines and double-jointed drive shafts. From 1971, the engine lid gained additional air louvres to aid engine cooling, and in 1972 a metal hood frame replaced the wood and metal frame used previously. Curiously, contemporary classic car price guides value the MacPherson strut Beetles in both saloon and cabriolet forms well above the traditional torsion bar cars, which of course is good news for addicts of the latter.

Although the MacPherson strut saloons were dropped from the range after a relatively brief production run of just five years, the cabriolet contin-

The 1303 cabriolets have a large panoramic windscreen (above left) and a much heavier and more shapely frame. The torsion bar and 1302 MacPherson strut cabriolets (above) have a flat windscreen and a 'clean-cut' frame.

ued with this layout to the end, the car being badged simply as a 1303. One important difference between European and American specification is that the former used engine lids fitted with thermostatically-controlled flaps between 1976 and 1979. The American market was also treated to a very smart all-white limited edition 'Champagne' version in 1977. The two last Beetle cabriolets to be built at Osnabrück, finished on 10 January 1980, were also all-white, and the very last example now resides in the Karmann factory museum.

Above all else, the Beetle cabriolet can be distinguished from virtually all other convertibles by the quality of its hood. Those who have bitten hard into their knuckles upon learning of the cost of a genuine replacement item can console themselves with the knowledge that a new hood for a Golf cabriolet is almost twice as much. Drive a cabriolet with the hood up and it is almost impossible to tell that you are in a convertible. The hood is so well made that it is completely water-tight and wind-proof. Although the ravages of time will eventually take their toll, it is also very durable. For most of its life, the exterior

vinyl material and plastic headlining contained a heavy horsehair and rubber padding, but a more modern foam material was used from 1976. Sadly, the biggest threat to the hood these days comes not from the weather but from vandals who appear to take great delight in slashing the vulnerable material. Short of equipping your car with security cameras, there is little you can do to prevent such mindless acts of barbarism.

For cabriolet restorers, there's good news and bad news. The good news is that around 70-80 per cent of the components that make up one of these coach-built beauties are still available from Volkswagen dealers, but the bad news is that they are far from cheap. Hood covers are still available for all cabriolets, but unfortunately frames are available from official outlets only for the 1303 curved-windscreen models. It goes without saying that the parts situation will deteriorate as the years go by, but at the time of writing cabriolet enthusiasts can consider themselves very lucky indeed, and those with left-hand-drive cars are better off than those with right-hand-drive examples.

Before 1961, the badge applied to the right-hand front quarter panel was rectangular and read 'Karmann Kabriolett' (above far left), with one 'K' serving both words. After 1961, the badge was more shapely (above left) and simply read 'Karmann'.

OPTIONS & ACCESSORIES

Accessories have always been popular with Beetle owners, which is one reason why no two cars are completely alike. The period parts on Alan Barlow's 1960 Beetle include a chromed Volkswagen script on the bonnet, a badge bar, whitewall tyres, polished stone guards on the wings and sprung steel rods (also fixed to the wings) for warning the driver against manoeuvring too close to a kerb. In addition to the semaphore indicators, this car has been fitted retrospectively with American-spec flashing indicators on the front wings.

Almost from the very beginning, few Beetle owners could resist fitting accessories and appendages of one kind and another to their cars, even if it was only a radio. Into the 1950s, a large industry specialising in 'after-market' accessories grew up very quickly specifically to cater for the Beetle, the first of such companies having been founded in 1949 by an ex-Volkswagen employee called Karl Meier.

His company, Kamei, started by retrimming Beetle seats in bright fabrics and selling them to German Volkswagen dealers, and then quickly moved on to making 'add-on' seat covers. The business was an instant success, and over the next 30 years or so the Kamei name became almost synonymous with Volkswagen accessories.

One of the earliest and most enduring Kamei products was a parcel shelf that slotted into place behind the rear seat just below the back windows. It had the added advantage of concealing valuables from prying eyes and contributed significantly to insulating the interior from the noise of the engine. A small pull-up lid in the centre of the shelf ensured

easy access to the small luggage area beneath it.

A parcel shelf for front seat passengers appeared at around the same time and fitted below the dashboard. It was a particularly useful accessory and Meier sold thousands of them over the years. Inspired by its early successes, Kamei went on to make dozens of Beetle 'extras', some more beneficial than others. Items included a hand-operated extension for the reserve fuel tap (foot-operated on the showroom cars), a wastepaper basket that resembled a shuttlecock for mounting on the tunnel in front of the gear lever, the inevitable steering wheel glove, arm-, knee- and neck-rests, and – arguably the most useful of all in the early days – a large, flat, conventional accelerator pedal that fitted over the standard roller assembly. All of these accessories were particularly popular on the home market and are much sought-after by collectors today. Needless to say, genuine Kamei components are not cheap.

As time went by, Karl Meier's inventive mind 'wandered' all over the Beetle, inside and out, but one accessory that wasn't an immediate success was his chin spoiler. The prototype aerofoil, beautifully

The circular tool box that fits in front of the spare wheel is now highly sought-after, but, being rare, is far from cheap.

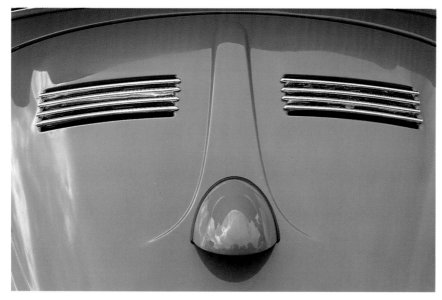

Chromed or stainless steel decorative grilles brighten up the engine lid louvres (above left), but have a tendency to trap moisture and cause corrosion. Extra chromed Volkswagen scripts (above) have made something of a comeback in recent years.

fashioned from aluminium alloy, resembled an aeroplane wing and was designed to fit below the bonnet. Not only was it aimed at making the Beetle more aerodymanically efficient, but also at reducing the car's instability in crosswinds. Meier took his aerofoil to the 1953 Geneva Motor Show, but sadly it was not taken seriously. The device was a long way ahead of its time and Meier shelved the idea for many years.

When in the 1970s Kamei eventually brought out a neater and altogether more practical chin spoiler made from plastic, Beetle drivers who fitted one reported an immediate improvement in directional stability in crosswinds. But when the Cal-look

became fashionable in Britain and Europe, Kamei spoilers decreased in popularity and have become a comparatively rare sight.

Kamei also marketed a neat plastic rest for the 'clutch foot' in the early 1950s. It was a particularly welcome addition on left-hand drive cars, but because of the manner in which the pedal cluster is arranged on right-hand drive Beetles, British owners had to do without this luxury.

One of the most popular items bought by Beetle folk during the 1950s was a flower vase that simply clipped or screwed to the dashboard. Available from a number of manufacturers, they were made in porcelain, steel and glass in a wide variety of designs

A rare steering wheel and additional instruments on this 1954 cabriolet are genuine Beetle accessories, but were not made by Volkswagen.

This 1954 car features a lift-up lever (right) to replace the standard rotary heater control knob. Car theft was a serious problem even in the 1950s and 1960s, but a gear lever lock (far right) deterred the majority of opportunists.

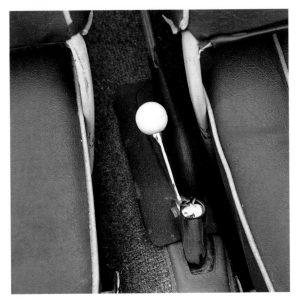

and colours. Original items today are again rare and likely to be expensive, but reproductions are available at reasonable cost. It goes without saying that a vase fitted to a Beetle should be replenished with fresh flowers – far nicer than the plastic ones often used by owners at shows – at every possible opportunity.

Radios always came as optional extras on Beetles and arguably the best sets were supplied by Blaupunkt. Renowned for their exceptional sound quality, Blaupunkt radios are unbelievably reliable and last for many years. Unhappily for people living in Britain, these wonderful period pieces have been rendered almost useless by the major radio networks that traditionally broadcasted on medium wave

transferring to FM.

Because of the limited power of six-volt head-lights, fog and spot lamps from Bosch and Hella were popular fitments from the early 1950s. Although they were externally well-made, their vulnerability to stone chips ensured that the lenses were easily broken, so these items are also rare today.

External bodywork embellishments from a variety of manufacturers over the years have included protective 'spats' (usually in aluminium alloy) for the front and rear wings, chrome-plated grilles that fit over the rear air-intake louvres, and – possibly the most bizarre of all – thin steel marker rods for placing vertically on the outside of the front wings in order to make parking and manoeuvring easier. In addition, there were chrome grilles for the bonnet fresh air vents (on post-1968 cars), chrome 'finger' plates to protect the paint behind the bonnet and door handles, and even a decorative grille to place over the two exhaust tail pipes.

Circular chrome-plated metal plugs were available for inserting in the jacking points, while a chrome-plated, fluted tail pipe extension was particularly popular in the 1950s. The headlamp 'eyelids', which gave the Beetle a rather sleepy appearance, were outlawed in Germany during the 1960s on the grounds that they presented a potential danger to pedestrians, but these quaint items have enjoyed a revival in

recent times despite the fact that they significantly reduce the car's top speed.

Rubber mud flaps were available through Volkswagen dealers with either a V-over-W emblem or a simplified representation of Wolfsburg Castle, both types of motif being in hard plastic. In Britain, the Speedwell company, of which the Grand Prix racing driver Graham Hill was a director, marketed a full range of accessories for Beetles, but most were aimed at the tuning market. To name but a few, there were tachometers, oil pressure and temperature gauges (usually fitted into the radio speaker panel to the side of the speedometer), stone guards for fitting below the headlights, and a rear anti-roll bar. Speedwell's

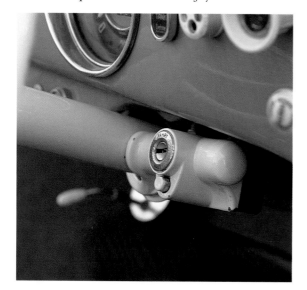

A column-mounted ignition switch and starter button (above left) were available in the 1950s. A fuel gauge (above) was available as an accessory during the 1950s before Volkswagen fitted one as standard equipment.

Not a Volkswagen accessory, but a picnic hamper in period style would never go amiss on long journeys.

Extensions for the gear lever and reserve petrol tap are both useful fittings which are not commonly seen today, whereas the parcel shelf is a popular addition. The flower vase is always a nice touch for 1950s and early 1960s cars, but would be incongruous on a later Beetle.

products were not officially sanctioned by Volkswagen, but they are worthy of mention because they played such a large role in the lives of would-be speed merchants by the mid-1960s.

As time went by, more and more equipment became available from both specialist companies and Volkswagen. By 1970, a prospective Beetle customer could spend almost as much money on accessories and extras as on a complete car. Volkswagen's sales brochures, expensive collectors' items in themselves, included long lists of optional extras which naturally differed from country to country.

In a typical model year, 1973 for example, the options offered by Volkswagen at extra cost included a radio, fog and spot lamps, towbar, mud flaps, additional exterior and interior trim, front parcel shelf, sports gear stick, tool kits and car care products.

By contrast, Volkswagen's list for the 1975 model year was almost never-ending, including a factory-fitted steel sliding sunroof, laminated windscreen, adjustable head restraints, radial tyres, twin reversing lights (standard with the 'L' package), inertia reel seat belts, radio, halogen headlights and automatic transmission on the 1300.

For the 1303 and cabriolet version in the same

model year, you could have front disc brakes, a sunroof with wind deflector, electric clock, radial tyres, radio, leatherette seats, head restraints, hinged-down armrest for the rear seat, rally steering wheel, heavy duty battery, 4½ or 5½J sports wheels, halogen headlights, rally seats, headlamp washers, reclining seats, two-speed fresh air blower, tinted windows and rubber bumper inserts – to name but a few.

However, for the 1978 model year, the last in which the Beetle was to be produced in Germany as a saloon, the Beetle reverted to basics. Factory-fitted extras were confined to a steel sliding sunroof and adjustable head restraints. At extra cost, dealers could 'only' supply fog and spot lamps, a rear fog lamp, mud flaps, a towbar, radio, central tunnel tray and storage trays.

The decision to fit any type of accessory comes down to personal preference. Inevitably, the more you fit, the heavier and more sluggish your car will become. Some accessories such as the wing spats, chrome grilles and bonnet 'bibs' have additional drawbacks. Whereas they certainly protect the paintwork against stone chips, they also have a tendency to trap condensation and can cause as much damage as they prevent.

BUYING & RESTORATION

With over 21 million Beetles having been made worldwide, there is certainly no shortage of choice on the second-hand market. If you are considering buying a Beetle, take your time before parting with hard-earned cash. Read all you can about the marque, join your local VW club, never be afraid to ask questions no matter how trivial they may seem, and always bear in mind that even the youngest German-made car is now 15 years old. Although the Beetle is able to resist corrosion better than most cars, neglected or well-used examples are almost bound to require costly attention sooner rather than later.

The days of stumbling across a low-mileage 'Split' or 'Oval' in pristine condition for £500 are over, so your decision to buy should be based on a realistic assessment of how much you can afford to spend. A Beetle in need of a full restoration, no matter how little the asking price, is going to be an expensive proposition, so it may make more sense to look for a really tidy and original or well-restored car from the outset. Such cars do exist, but they are becoming increasingly difficult to find.

Over the past 15 years or so, interest in the Beetle has increased dramatically all over the world with the result that many cars which would have otherwise been consigned to a scrap heap have attracted the attention of 'bodgers'. Apart from being offered for sale with a dubious certificate of roadworthiness and a shiny new paint job, such cars have very little to commend them.

Not surprisingly for a car that has been in production for around half a century, the Beetle has grown up surrounded by myth, but most of the criticism which has been aimed at these wonderful little cars is based, happily, on supposition and has little or no foundation in fact. Contrary to popular belief, well-maintained cars do not have lousy heaters that give out more in the way of exhaust fumes than warmth, they do not have awkwardly positioned pedals, and they are far from noisy. In truth, a Beetle fitted with genuine Volkswagen heat exchangers will comprehensively cook its occupants no matter how cold the weather, and cars which threaten the driver and his passengers with exhaust gases are those which have badly corroded or incorrectly fitted heat exchangers. Professor Porsche's design for his People's car was conceived to bring affordable and enjoyable motoring to people like you and I. He most certainly did not set out to commit genocide by incorporating an exhaust system capable of causing carbon monoxide poisoning.

Inferior roadholding and handling are the other two most popularly misconceived ideas which are said to set the Beetle aside from the common herd. The cars certainly have a rear weight bias, but this simply means that conducting a Beetle safely around a corner at high speed demands a different driving technique which, once learned and practised, is delightful and rewarding in the extreme as any seasoned campaigner will confirm. Porsche expected the same standard of driving from his customers as they did of his engineering.

The Volkswagen became popular in the 1950s and

Removing the body from the chassis pan is not a task to be undertaken lightly, but is inevitable if the sills are badly rusted.

1960s for many reasons. Behind the happy smiling face, legendary reliability, good fuel economy and unique styling, there was, above all else, an aura of exceptional build quality rarely seen in other makes even to this day. And although it may seem anomalous, the older the Beetle, the better the quality is likely to be.

On that basis, it would be sensible to buy a 'Split' or an 'Oval', but there are drawbacks to these models: you will have to content yourself with six-volt electrics, semaphore indicators, comparatively poor engine performance and limited all-round visibility. The owner of a Beetle from the late 1960s or early 1970s, on the other hand, will certainly experience improved handling, more power and better lighting, but arguably a lot less in the way of character. It is also worth taking into consideration the fact that spare parts are more readily available for the post-1967 12-volt cars. Partly because Beetle production continues to this day in Mexico, spare parts are also relatively inexpensive, which is one reason why restoring and running a Beetle still makes extremely good sense.

WHAT TO LOOK FOR

The condition of the bodywork should be of prime consideration as mechanical components are, in most cases, easy to find and cheap to replace. Rust most commonly attacks the bottom six inches or so and particular attention should be paid to the sills, jacking points, floorpan, inner wings, front and rear quarter panels, the bottoms of the doors, spare wheel well and the front and rear bumper hangers. Repair panels are available for all these vulnerable areas but fitting them may prove expensive if you do not have the skill or equipment to do it yourself.

If you are considering a car which its owner has already restored, ask to see a photographic record of the work as it progressed, especially if the work carried out is recent. And again, do not be fooled by a shiny new paint job – it could be hiding a host of horrors underneath. By the same token, a fresh layer of wax polish may be hiding minor blemishes in the paint, so take a good look into that deep shine for evidence of scratches. It is also useful to talk at length with the vendor not only about his car but about Volkswagens in general. The conversation will reveal, if nothing else, whether or not he or she is an enthusiast who really cares about Beetles.

If the sills are very rusty, the only satisfactory means of repair is complete replacement with new panels for which the body must be removed from the floorpan. In recent times, it has become customary to leave the body in place and weld new sills to the floorpan, which must be considered unacceptable on the grounds that Porsche never intended it that way. In addition, if the doors 'drop' when opened oversize hinge pins will probably have to be fitted.

The overall condition of the interior will also offer a reasonably good idea as to how the car has been treated. Although Volkswagen fixtures and fittings are very durable, the headlining and seats are vulnerable to the wear and tear of everyday use. A collapsed

The body panels of this 1952 'Split' are in exceptionally good condition, but there is corrosion damage around the windows. Sandblasting down to bare metal is the only practical solution in an area like this where a grinding tool cannot be used.

and sagging driver's seat will give you the best clue towards establishing a car's true mileage. I once answered an advertisement for what was described as a 'low-mileage 1965 1200 Beetle in excellent condition' only to discover that the truth was completely the opposite. Apart from a broken headlamp, scruffy paintwork and rusty sills, the driver's seat had collapsed in the middle which inevitably meant that the 32,000 miles indicated on the odometer was in fact more likely to have been 132,000 or even 232,000.

Lift up the rear seat cushion and check the state of the floorpan beneath the battery, a common site for advanced corrosion. At the same time, it's worth making a note of the chassis number which is stamped on top of the backbone between the two floorpan halves (except on the early cars) to ensure that it correlates with the information on the registration document. Search also in the luggage space behind the rear seat for evidence of damp. Water leaking through the rear window rubber seal is a common problem on older cars and will eventually cause rot in the horizontal panel which forms the base of the luggage compartment. The rear inner wings which protrude into the car's interior should come in for careful scrutiny at the same time because rust in this region requires major surgery.

Mechanically, Beetles are among the most durable and rugged motor cars ever made, but that is not to say that they never break or wear out. Naturally, a car with a full service history is desirable, if a little unlikely these days, but in the absence of documentation it will soon become apparent as to whether or not the car is in good shape simply by driving it and listening to the engine.

Before turning the ignition key, take a look in the engine bay and under the engine itself. Look for petrol leaks from the carburettor (an indication of wear in the throttle spindle) and evidence of oil leaks. Is everything tidy and clean or is there filth and grime everywhere? Does the engine number stamped on the crankcase below the generator pedestal tie up with the one in the vehicle's registration document? Are the pushrods leaking oil? Most do on old engines, but a small amount is by no means serious.

Check for holes in the heat exchangers, particularly around the area where they join the tailbox. Serious rusting here will allow exhaust fumes into the car and genuine replacements are expensive. Naturally, a test drive will give you the best indication as to the car's overall mechanical condition. A good Beetle should feel taut and lively and ought to bring a smile to your face instantly. A bad one probably won't. Blue smoke from the tailpipes when the engine is started is usually indicative of worn valve gear unless the car has been parked on a slope, in which case it is perfectly normal.

Common faults which will normally rear their

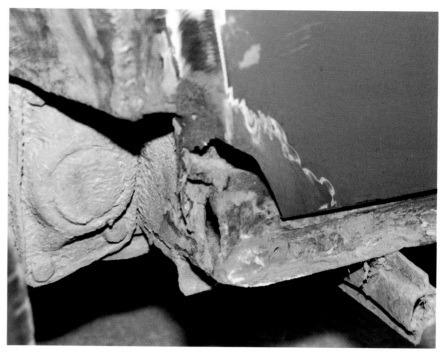

heads while out on the road include an inclination to wander (which can usually be traced to worn steering components such as the ball joints/kingpins or steering boxes/racks) and a tendency on high mileage cars to jump out of gear (which either means worn synchromesh or that it's time to change the rubber gearbox mountings). A Beetle that will not travel satisfactorily in a straight line may just be sitting on crossply tyres, in which case make a note to change to radials at the earliest opportunity. From a safety point of view, the world's entire complement of crossplies, as fitted to Beetles, should all be gathered together in one large warehouse and kept *ad infinitum* under house arrest. For those who would prefer to forsake safety in favour of originality, the very best of luck to you.

Once satisfied that the car is sound or is as least in sufficiently good condition to allow you to stay within your restoration budget, go ahead and write out the cheque.

RESTORATION

One great advantage of restoring a Beetle lies in the simplicity of the car's construction. The wings are bolted to the body and the body is bolted to the chassis pan. Obviously, for the sake of retaining originality, it is desirable to preserve as many parts as possible, even though buying a set of new wings is invariably cheaper in the long run than repairing the existing ones.

Repair panels are readily available for the bottoms of the doors, front and rear quarter panels, sills, front apron and inner wings. There is only one way of fitting them: the correct way. Taking a new door skin,

When the rear quarter panels rust through, the only course of action is to cut out the original metal and weld in a new panel. To smooth out the join between the two panels, lead-loading is preferable to body filler, but needs to be carried out by a skilled craftsman if costly mistakes are to be avoided.

The rear inner wings are particularly vulnerable to corrosion, but repair panels are readily and cheaply available.

Although badly rusted, the two halves of the floorpan on this early 'Split' will need sandblasting as a precaution against the return of rust, but first the original steering wheel, gear lever knob and choke button must be removed to prevent them from being ruined by the blasting process.

welding it over the top of the old rusty one and smoothing it all out with body filler is not correct, but is a particularly popular method with bodgers whose three score years and ten would be better served in catching rats.

Rust commonly attacks the rain channels along the seam welds and, in cases of advanced corrosion where a grinding tool will not do the job satisfacto-

rily, shotblasting may provide the answer. Dipping the entire bodyshell in an acid bath is the surest way of eradicating rust but is generally expensive and largely unnecessary. The same applies to the floorpan. It is extremely rare for the backbone tunnel to rot out completely but the two halves of the floorpan are vulnerable. If they can't be saved, new ones are readily and cheaply available. Patching up dozens of holes is acceptable unless you are preparing your car for concours d'elegance. Having cleaned and thoroughly de-rusted the chassis, it is very tempting to reach for a tin of black Hammerite: as good at resisting corrosion as this product undoubtedly is, the 'crackle' finish is neither original nor especially pleasant to look at.

One excellent product in which all restorers should invest is Waxoyl. It does not look pretty once it dries, but it does help to repel moisture. If sprayed, brushed or trickled into every nook and cranny, it will instil a glowing sense of confidence that your pride and joy is not rotting away once again. Incidentally, Waxoyl has a tendency to dry out and crack over a period of time, so the treatment ought really to be repeated annually. Years ago, people used to treat the underside of the floorpan with old engine oil by applying it with a brush, but apart from the fact that oil never lasts very long, it also has a nasty tendency to run down your arm, giving a wholly new meaning to the expression 'elbow grease'. Waxoyl is not only better but is also user-friendly.

It is also a good idea to apply Waxoyl to the under-

Virtually all the parts necessary to rebuild a post-1967 12-volt Beetle are available from Mexico, including complete bodyshells. The roof panel in the foreground is the very last to be made by Volkswagen in Germany.

side of the wings, rear valance and spare wheel well. Although dust sticks to it, it is surely preferable to rust. Incidentally, when the waistline brightwork is removed, it is quite easy to bend it slightly so that there is a small gap between the trim and the bodywork when you refit it. If that does happen, a smear of Waxoyl or Vaseline is a good idea on a regular basis to prevent water being trapped and causing corrosion. Vaseline can also be used to protect the bumpers, headlight rims and other chromed parts, especially through the winter months, but again it picks up dust and does not look especially pleasant.

If restoring the body is relatively easy, the interior, and more particularly the upholstery and headlining, will prove a little more tricky. Frankly, both jobs are best left to a professional trimmer. Because there are

a number of Beetles still languishing in scrapyards, good seats are still obtainable cheaply, although the rear backrests of the vinyl items fitted to nearly all Beetles throughout the 1960s and 1970s have a tendency to split along their top edge. The cheapest solution to this perennial problem is a strategically placed piece of sticky tape but such a crude move will certainly not find favour with concours judges.

Steering wheels and instruments are in plentiful supply, and the best hunting grounds are Volkswagen shows and autojumbles. So many Beetles have been fitted with smaller-than-standard steering wheels that the original items are available by the bucket load. Obviously, you can expect to pay more for a three-spoke wheel for an early 'Split'.

Mechanically, Beetles present few problems over

Rebuilding an engine to Volkswagen's original standard is best left to professionals. This reconditioned 30bhp single-port 1200 power unit (above left) retains its original crankshaft, camshaft, crankcase and cylinder heads. Despite appearances that suggest serious corrosion (above), this floorpan has a light coating of surface rust, but for additional peace of mind it will need sandblasting prior to painting.

With the bonnet, wings and doors removed, the extent to which the body has corroded can be assessed more easily. This 1951 'Split' (right) has been partially painted with lead oxide to prevent further corrosion while repairs are carried out to the rest of the car. Rebuilding the engine and other mechanicals should be left till last (far right).

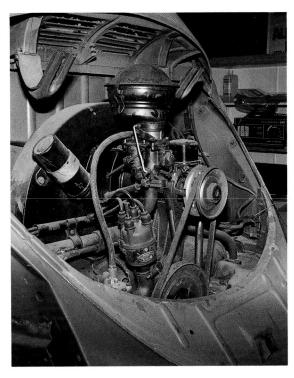

availability of parts. The later engines can be obtained on an exchange basis or purchased outright from mainly independent specialists, but scrapyards and autojumbles are a good source if you are on a tighter budget. Almost every fellow VW enthusiast these days will be able to help out if you are stuck for an engine because the majority appear to have at least one spare unit in the garage or, more likely, in the airing cupboard.

From the point of view of originality, it would always be preferable to retain the engine that is original to your car. Rebuilding your own engine from scratch is not especially difficult if you have a good working knowledge of the intricacies of internal combustion. Naturally, it is desirable to fit new parts when doing so, but it is relatively rare to find second-hand crankshafts and camshafts, for example, that are so badly worn as to be unworthy of further service. A new set of pistons and barrels is a good idea and they are cheap, but a new set of piston rings may well suffice. A few years ago, Simon Woodall, a well-known exponent of the art of VW trialling, built an engine for fun using pistons and barrels from a 1200, 1300, 1500 and 1600 engine, and, strangely enough, it worked. Beetle engines are so tough and strong that short of filling the combustion chambers with molten lead, it's difficult not to make them work.

Conversely, gearboxes are a definite 'no-go' area except for an acknowledged expert. Designed and over-engineered to accept power units of up to around 150bhp, Volkswagen gearboxes are extremely reliable for many thousands of miles but when a replacement is needed the least expensive route is a secondhand unit, which is not difficult to locate.

Attempting to rebuild your original one without specialist knowledge and equipment will almost certainly end in tears, so it's probably best not to try.

Generally, the suspension components of the traditional torsion bar cars are very long-lived indeed and usually require little in the way of restoration. Torsion bars can snap if they are abused, but such occurrences are rare and replacements are available anyway. The front uprights that locate the top of the shock absorbers are vulnerable to corrosion and should be checked carefully for holes. Both small and large areas of advanced corrosion can be plated, but the results are seldom pretty. If you're in any doubt about the quality of the welding work, a replacement front beam should be fitted sooner rather than later. It is simply not worth taking risks over safety, especially as a new beam costs considerably less than a decent colour television.

CONCLUSION

Throughout the course of restoration work, there will be times when you feel that you should not have started in the first place. The sheer frustration of trying to remove rusty nuts and bolts, the pain of hitting your knuckles when a spanner slips, the mess on the garage floor, the expense of it all and the seemingly never-ending nature of the work will almost certainly drive you to despair on occasions. But take heart. We have all felt like that, but the sense of elation after months or years of hard work more than compensates for the aches and pains. And, when you have finally finished, enjoy driving your Beetle because that is what Porsche intended it for.

ACKNOWLEDGEMENTS

THE AUTHOR

Grateful thanks are due to the following people for their help: Bob Shaill, Dr Simon Parkinson, George Shetliffe, Peter Stevens, Bill Jennings, Suzie King, Major Ivan Hirst, Chris Bosley, Elizabeth Harvey, Howard Cheese, Julian Meredith and Ilse Bohn.

The author also wishes to express his gratitude to Charles Herridge and Mark Hughes for their kindness and encouragement.

THE EDITOR

For allowing their splendid Beetles to be photographed for this book, sincere appreciation is due to the following: Hermann Walter, Peter Colborne-Baber, Paul Hough, Dave Cantle, John Maxwell, Howard Chadwick, Dr Simon Parkinson, Nick Carr-Forster, Eva Miller, Alan Barlow, Danny Hermans, Graham Smith, Jo Clay, Bob Wynn, Gordon Sellars, Stuart Andrews, John Alexander, Julie Kaye, Pascal Knockaert, Vic Kaye, Roger Slim, Rob Loughrey, Will Shaw and VAG (United Kingdom) Ltd.

Besides some of those enthusiasts already mentioned, additional help in locating the cars was provided by Rod Sleigh. Although Paul Debois took the vast majority of the photographs in this book, the work of Brigitte Wegner, Laurence Meredith and Richard Sealey is also featured.